Really Reading!

Really Reading!

10 Simple and Effective Methods to Develop Your Child's Love for Reading

Janet Gardner
&
Lora Myers

ADAMS MEDIA CORPORATION
Holbrook, Massachusetts

Permissions on the copyright page continue on page 157.

Published by Adams Media Corporation
260 Center Street, Holbrook, MA 02343

ISBN: 1-55850-708-6

Printed in Canada.

J I H G F E D C B

Library of Congress-in-Publication Data
Gardner, Janet.
Really reading! : 10 simple and effective methods to develop your child's love
for reading! / Janet Gardner & Lora Myers
      p.   cm.
ISBN 1-55850-708-6 (pb)
1. Reading—Parent participation. 2. Children—Books and reading.
I. Myers, Lora. II. Title.
LB1050.2.G37   1997
372.4—dc21   96-54818
                                  CIP

Photo courtesty of ©The Stock Market/Lew Long, 1995.

*This book is available at quantity discounts for bulk purchases.
For information, call 1-800-872-5627 (in Massachusetts, 617-767-8100).*

Visit our home page at http://www.adamsmedia.com

Many thanks to the librarians in the Children's Room at the Katonah Village Library, for whom the words *pleasant* and *helpful* were invented.

Contents

Getting Started

What Is Really Reading?

A young mother and her three-year-old daughter are seated in a sunny corner of the children's room of their local public library. The mother has picked out an award-winning picture book and is reading it to her child with enthusiasm. Every once in a while, she interrupts herself to ask: "Are you listening? Are you listening?"

At a nearby table, a boy of about six reads aloud to his father from a book about going to the moon. The child reads pretty well, although with very little expression. Every once in a while, when the boy turns the page, his dad says, "Good."

What is going on here?

We are watching two parents who are trying hard to help their children, but who are not really getting the job done. Like many of us, they are reading with their children on a regular basis. They may also be teaching them to sound out letters and recognize whole words. They think all this will ensure that their kids will become agile, competent readers who love to read.

However, while all these things are important, they are not enough. These parents, like many others, are missing out on great opportunities to teach their children how to *really read*.

What is Real Reading? First and foremost, unlike watching television, reading is not meant to be a passive activity. Real Readers are *active*, *engaged*, *alert readers* whose brains are working all the time. They don't just sit staring off into space while somebody reads to them. They don't just drone on without thinking about what they are reading. Real Readers call upon a variety of skills that enable them to read with pleasure and to get the most out of what they read.

Children who tell us they don't like to read are telling us something important. They are really saying that they don't have the skills they need to enjoy reading. In other words, they have not mastered the skills of Real Readers—what reading teachers call *comprehension* and *critical thinking skills*.

Helping your child develop comprehension and critical thinking skills just sounds complicated. The good news is that it isn't, and you don't need a Ph.D. in education to do it. You just need to tuck one or more of these ten easy-to-learn, easy-to-use *Really Reading!* strategies into regular reading time.

Really Reading! strategies are playful, powerful techniques used by professionals—and savvy parents—to turn every reading session into a focused and dynamic learning experience. You can apply *Really Reading!* techniques to all kinds of reading material, from fairy tales to fables, poems to biographies, letters to e-mail, without worrying that you are taking the fun out of reading. On the contrary, *Really Reading!* strategies help make every story livelier and less predictable—even the one you're reading for the zillionth time. You'll never have to ask, "Are you listening?"

Of course, there's nothing wrong and a lot right with simply reading a story to the sleepy little girl or boy on your lap. However, when you read that very same story the *Really Reading!* way, you are making the most of your reading time together. You are helping your young reader develop important habits of mind that apply to learning tasks of all kinds, from taking tests to writing reports to working on a computer.

Without *Really Reading!* strategies, a child cannot become a Real Reader. However, most schools do not focus on comprehension and critical thinking skills until the second half of second grade, when reading problems become obvious and sabotage academic performance and self-esteem. Yet educators agree that academic ability begins to be shaped by age three!

It's up to us, our children's first teachers, to give our kids a head start.

Real Readers Know How To:

- Predict what is likely to happen next
- Figure out unfamiliar words
- Recognize different types of reading material
- Retell what they've read in their own words
- See different points of view
- Read between the lines
- Get the main idea
- Use their imaginations
- Create their own stories
- Think about what books they like and what books they don't

How to Really Read with Your Child

When you ride a bike, you have to do lots of things. You have to keep your balance. You have to pedal, steer, brake, and look and think ahead so you don't run into a tree. Even though you are doing all these things—some of them at the same time, some of them in sequence—once you have become a good bike rider you don't think about any of these skills. After a while, riding starts to feel easy and is more fun. But if you find riding a bike hard, you'll never relax and enjoy it.

Real Reading is like riding a bicycle. For readers who are just starting out, the many skills involved in reading do not come easily. They have no time to look around and enjoy the scenery. Yet parents who don't think twice about helping their kids become good bike riders often neglect to help them practice and master important comprehension and critical thinking skills.

Think of yourself as your young reader's training wheels! When you read together, your child should not be sitting like a lump while you rush to turn the page. To make sure that your beginning reader becomes an active reader, you need to think of reading as a participatory activity. The mother at the library who kept asking "Are you listening?"

sensed that her little girl had lost interest, but she didn't know how to keep her child's attention focused on the book. The father who just kept saying "Good" unknowingly sent the message that all you have to do is get the words right. A *Really Reading!* strategy or two would have solved this problem.

Really Reading! techniques make reading more active by prompting you and your child to think and talk about what you are reading in ways that enhance the reading experience. It's as simple as that.

Over time, your young reader will start to do by himself some of the things you have been *modeling*—that is, showing him how to do. Just as you can model good manners by being polite yourself, when you use *Really Reading!* techniques, you are modeling the kind of reading behavior that will result in increased comprehension and a love of reading.

When you use this book, keep these tips in mind:

RELAX

"I'm not a reading teacher!" you may be thinking. "It's been years since I was in school! How can I possibly teach my child to read?"

Don't worry. This book was written for people who haven't thought about reading since they learned to read themselves. Each *Really Reading!* technique is explained step-by-step, with lots of examples. After a little practice, you'll start to feel like a reading expert.

BEGIN WHEN YOU THINK YOUR CHILD IS READY

As with other developmental skills, we have come to understand that children come to reading in different ways and over different periods of time. The child who catches on to *Really Reading!* techniques early does not necessarily turn out to be a better reader than the child who catches on later. With a little trial and error, you will soon find the right time to begin using *Really Reading!* techniques when you read with your youngster.

Don't feel you have to apply every one of the *Really Reading!* techniques every single time you read. There will be many moments when your child is so absorbed that you will not want to interrupt the flow of the story. Take the cue from your young reader. Your goal is to enhance his or her reading pleasure, not detract from it. You can always use a technique or two after you've read the story or the next time you read it.

CHOOSE YOUR STRATEGY

Really Reading! strategies are loosely organized by level of difficulty. Easier skills, like vocabulary and prediction, come first. More complex skills, like inference and identifying the main idea, follow.

Although Real Readers usually use many of these techniques at the same time, we have separated them so you can practice them more easily and help your child master each one. You'll find that as your child becomes more experienced and these skills become second nature, they get rolled up into one all-purpose ball. Without having to think about it, your Real Reader will begin to pick and choose what he needs in order to increase reading understanding and enjoyment.

Take into account the age and development of your young reader and tuck a strategy or two into reading time. Start with the easier skills. If your child doesn't seem enthusiastic, back off and try another time. Your cue will come from your youngster's attention span, verbal ability, and body language (the fidget-and-squirm factor). Try again in a couple of weeks, or a month or two. In a short time, young children make great developmental strides.

When you feel your child has mastered one technique, such as predicting, introduce another, such as using context clues to build vocabulary. Soon you will find that you are using several techniques. Think of them as ingredients: the more you add, the more delicious the reading experience.

START WITH BOOKS THAT APPEAL TO YOU

Until you find out what your child likes to read, select books that you loved when you were small and new stories that strike your fancy. Your child is especially likely to enjoy a book that you get a kick out of yourself.

If you can't think of any beloved books, spend a little time in the children's room of your local library. Ask the librarian to suggest authors and titles children love. You can also get good ideas from many lists of recommended children's books, such as *The New York Times Parent's Guide to the Best Books for Children*.

VARY THE KINDS OF BOOKS YOU READ

There's nothing wrong with reading a child's favorite tale over and over, and very small children will demand it. You should try, however, to vary the reading menu. There's so much good stuff out there—from fairy tales to fables, poetry to pop-ups, biographies to books on biology—and your young reader should be exposed to all of it.

MAKE READING A HABIT

Reading is a habit you want to encourage. To get your child hooked, you need to establish a regular, focused time for reading.

While it's nice to set aside a leisurely time each day to sit and read together, this may not always be possible. There's no point in feeling guilty if you don't have large blocks of time to read with your child. Just remember that some reading time every single day is better than no reading time!

How much is "some reading time?" Fifteen minutes a day is fine, or whatever it takes to read a whole story or chapter. If you only have five minutes to spare, put off reading off until a better moment. It's important to give the young reader a chance to settle down a little and focus. If you're always reading on the fly, you are probably making a child's short attention span even shorter.

MODEL GOOD READING BEHAVIOR

No matter how tired you are, try not to drone! Put your heart into reading! Let the actor in you emerge! If you sound bored, you can't expect your child to be interested.

Pay attention to your pace. It's a good idea to read something new or difficult a little more slowly than you would an old favorite.

Children often learn more from what their parents do than what they say. Your child watches you when you read. If you don't seem to be enjoying yourself, you are sending a message that reading isn't much fun.

IF YOUR CHILD CAN READ, TAKE TURNS READING

As your children mature, encourage them to read to you—ideally, with lots of expression! "Reading" can also mean

asking a very young child to *tell* you a familiar story as you flip the pages.

USE *REALLY READING!* STRATEGIES WITH EVERYBODY

If you're a parent with more than one young reader in the house, don't worry. Even if you sit down to read with three children of different ages (or triplets!) at three different levels of reading interest and ability, each child can participate at his own level. These strategies are helpful to readers of all ages.

BROWSE THE *REALLY READING!* BOOKSHELF

There are books that work especially well with specific *Really Reading!* strategies. As you become familiar with the strategies, you are going to get good at identifying stories that match up well with specific skills.

The *Really Reading!* Bookshelf, an expanded list of books that work well with *Really Reading!* techniques, and Books Discussed, books used as examples in each chapter, appear at the end of the book.

BORROW BOOKS

Real Readers go the library every chance they get. Get into the habit of taking your children to the library.

BUY BOOKS

A Real Reader has a home library. Give a book for every birthday and every holiday. Encourage friends and relatives to do the same. When you go out shopping and your child asks for a treat, buy a book!

The very best gift you can give your child is the gift of reading. Most children's books are cheaper than toys and a far better investment in your child's future.

PART two:

The Ten *Really Reading!* Strategies

1 Guess What Happens Next!

SKILL: PREDICTING

"Don't go into Mr. McGregor's garden!" Mrs. Rabbit warns her four little rabbits, Flopsy, Mopsy, Cotton-tail, and Peter, in the *The Tale of Peter Rabbit* by Beatrix Potter . . . and right away the Real Reader suspects that at least one little bunny is going to disobey his mother and get himself into hot water.

Every time Real Readers pick up a book, they peek into the future. First, they check out the cover and predict what the story's about. Then, as they read on, they pay attention to helpful clues and use them to try to figure out what is likely to happen. As they read, Real Readers ask themselves the eternal question: *What happens next?*

Practicing prediction sets a young reader on the path to becoming an active reader.

It's fun to make the right prediction; this makes a reader feel smart. Your child is likely to remember what she's read if the story works out as she thought it would.

It's fun to get a big surprise if a tale takes an unexpected twist. You are likely to remember what you've read if something happens that you didn't anticipate.

Whether your prediction turns out to be right or wrong, you're more likely to remember what you read if you have been anticipating, that is, *thinking ahead* as you read.

Real Readers learn to grasp the shape and structure of a book by tuning in to repeated patterns. They realize early on that three can be a pretty magical number—after all, there are three bears and three little pigs and three blind mice. Characters get three wishes; kings and queens have three beautiful daughters or three handsome sons; fairy tale princesses have three suitors. It doesn't take long for Real Readers to start predicting that something special is likely to happen the third time around. The third pig will defeat the wolf; the third suitor will win the princess; the third wish will be the one that does the trick.

In addition to developing expectations about shape and structure, Real

Readers use the skill of prediction to guess how characters are likely to behave. It is usually the youngest prince or princess who is the bravest and who saves the day. A character who is described as "poor but honest" may do something foolish, but he is not going to do something sneaky. Peter Rabbit is going to get into trouble because, as the author tells us, he's a "very naughty" bunny who never listens to his mother, even though she warns him that Mr. McGregor captured Peter's father and baked him into a pie. The reader who foresees that Peter will sneak into Mr. McGregor's garden anyway is absolutely right.

Children develop so many useful reading skills when they practice predicting that books for even the very youngest readers include loads of predictable patterns. Take a look at a half-dozen preschool books and you'll quickly see that many of them feature repeated phrases or themes so that children can learn to anticipate. For example, in Eric Carle's *The Very Lonely Firefly*, a young firefly searches for others of his kind but is fooled time and again—first by a lightbulb, then by a candle, then by a lantern, and so on. At the end of the book, as you might predict, he finds his own true brothers and sisters.

Some books make it especially easy for a reader to start predicting before the first page is turned. For example, Robert Lawson's drawing on the cover of *The Story of Ferdinand* by Munro Leaf shows Ferdinand, a bull with powerful shoulders and massive horns, sniffing a flower which he holds with his daintily raised hoof.

This picture tells us a lot about Ferdinand, for bulls are usually fierce and quarrelsome, not gentle flower lovers. As we read on, we have to keep in mind what we've observed about Ferdinand because this will help in predicting what is going to happen.

The first time you read a book:

Look at the title and the cover illustration together.

Prompt your child to talk about them.

Ask: What do you think this book is about? Do you understand all the words in the title? What do you think is going to happen? Does this look like a sad or a happy book? What makes you think so?

Read aloud. If your child can read, take turns reading.

Choose opportunities in the story to prompt the reader to look ahead. As we read on in *The Story of Ferdinand*, we see that all the other bulls love to fight and can't wait to be picked to face a matador in the bull ring. Ferdinand, however, is not a typical bull. He only likes to sit quietly and smell the flowers.

Ask: Do you think Ferdinand wants to be chosen to fight in the bull ring? Why or why not? How do you know? (If your child says yes, Ferdinand wants to go with the other bulls, you might want to go back and reread before going on.) What do you think is going to happen next? (Keep reading and you'll see!)

Prompt your young reader to think about clues in the story and to make educated guesses based on new information as the writer provides it.

Don't rush in with answers. Give the reader time to cast a line into the future and reel in the possibilities.

Readers who practice predicting learn how to:

◆ Think ahead
◆ Pay attention to details about the plot and the characters
◆ Pay attention to patterns and sequence
◆ Draw logical conclusions

Example #1

Let's say you're reading *The Three Little Pigs* to your child for the first time. There are many variations on this story. In a typical version, the big bad wolf, who is intent on having pork for dinner, blows down the first little pig's flimsy house of straw and makes quick work of gobbling up the homeowner. Afterward, the wolf decides he wants another helping. He heads for the second little pig's house, which is made of sticks.

Ask: What do you think the wolf is going to do now? Do you think a house of sticks is stronger than a house of straw? What is the second little pig going to do?

Praise the child who succeeds in predicting the next step of the story.

Say: Good guess! Why did you think that was going to happen?

If the reader imagines a different outcome, do not treat this as a mistake. Decide whether this is a good time to go back and look for missed clues

OR

Say: I like your idea, but this is a different story. Let's see what happens next.

Now read on.

The house of sticks proves to be no stronger than the house of straw, and the wolf easily blows it down and eats up the second little pig. But the wolf is still hungry. He decides to head over to the home of the third little pig, which is made of bricks.

Ask: What is the wolf going to do now? Do you think the house of bricks is stronger than the house of straw? Do you think the wolf will be able to blow it down? What do you think the third little pig will do?

After the child guesses,

Say: Let's read on and see what happens.

At the end of the story, praise the child who has made good predictions ("You were right!"), but **don't criticize** if your child comes up with a different ending ("Look, it has a different ending than we thought. It was a good guess, though!").

Remember not to push too hard if she's simply not getting it. You might want to wait a few months before trying again.

Example #2

In *The Paperbag Princess* by Robert Munsch, a dragon captures a prince and sets fire to the kingdom. His fiancée, a spirited princess, comes up with a plan to trick the dragon and rescue the prince. She asks the dragon to prove over and over again that he can fly around the world in a split second.

Ask: Why do you think the princess wants the dragon to keep flying? (To tire him out.) What will happen to the dragon? (He will fall asleep.) What is the princess trying to do? (Rescue the prince while the dragon is sleeping.) Do you think she will rescue her prince? (She does.) What do you think will happen next? (In this story, the princess does **not** marry the prince, who is an ungrateful bum!)

Example #3

"The Elephant's Child," from Rudyard Kipling's classic *Just So Stories*, introduces an inquisitive elephant who annoys just about everybody in the jungle with his constant questions.

One morning, the Elephant's Child asks a new question which particularly upsets the other animals: "What does the Crocodile have for dinner?"

Ask: What is it that the Elephant's Child wants to know? Why do you think the other animals get upset when he asks this question? How would you answer the Elephant's Child if he asked you, "What does the Crocodile have for dinner?"

Read on and follow the Elephant's Child to the banks of the great, gray-green greasy Limpopo River, where the Crocodile lurks.

Praise the reader who figures out what the other animals know— that the Crocodile eats foolish young elephants and almost every other creature that crosses his path!

If your child guesses something else—banana stew, for example— that's okay, too. She'll find out the awful truth soon enough. At the end of the story, you may want to remind her why the other animals were so upset by the Elephant Child's question. They feared he would end up in the Crocodile's stomach.

Example #4

For a more advanced reader, turn the spotlight on the characters. In *Pinocchio: the Story of a Puppet* by Carlo Collodi, a poor woodcarver named Gepetto creates a wooden puppet, Pinocchio, who longs to be a real boy. But Pinocchio has naughty habits which stand in his way. He runs away and falls in with bad company—a dishonest duo, the fox and the cat. He also tells lies; however, since his nose grows when he lies, he can't get away with it. The moral of the long and entertaining story is that only by changing his behavior can Pinocchio become human and a real son to Gepetto.

Explain that a character can be a person, an animal, or a thing; for example, Gepetto, the fox, or Pinocchio, respectively.

Ask: What do you think of Pinocchio? Is he kind or mean, smart or silly, brave or cowardly? (Pinocchio is foolish and does not obey his father.) What is Gepetto like? (Gepetto is good-hearted but stern.) What do you think of the fox and the cat? (The fox and the cat pretend to be Pinocchio's friends, but they are up to no good.)

Use all the clues, including the characters' names and the pictures, if any, to figure out what the characters are like.

Predict how they are likely to behave, based on what you know about them. For example, your child may guess that because Pinocchio is foolish, he will be tricked out of his money by the greedy fox and cat.

Now read on, and discover whether the characters behave as expected.

Example #5

This next story requires a little imagination to predict how two characters will solve a problem. *Mrs. Piggle-Wiggle's Magic*, by Betty MacDonald, is one of a series of delightful books about a lovable witch who is the perfect mother's helper. In magical ways, Mrs. Piggle-Wiggle can teach a messy eater to mind his table manners and a "never-want-to-go-to-schooler" to love learning.

One day, an exasperated mom asks Mrs. P. to cure her bratty son and daughter of the horrible disease of *tattletaleitis*. After swallowing a few of Mrs. Piggle-Wiggle's mysterious black pills, the children discover that whenever they tattle on one another, a smoky black cloud, trailing a tail for each tattle, flies out of their mouths and hangs over their heads. How can the children get rid of these embarrassing tattle-tails?

Ask: How are the children going to make the black clouds go away?

Focus attention on this clue: Mrs. Piggle-Wiggle's goal is to make the children stop tattling. Your child should keep this in mind as she makes her prediction.

Read on. See how Mrs. Piggle-Wiggle solves the problem.

Did you come up with a different answer? (You'll have to read the book to find out what happens.)

With practice, your young reader will learn how to predict how a character is likely to act in different situations, notice if a character's behavior changes, and revise ideas about a character in response to new information.

FOLLOW-UP

Predicting can continue even when a story is over. Keep asking questions that point to the future and spark your child's imagination. Some follow-up questions for books discussed in this chapter are:

For *The Tale of Peter Rabbit:* What do you think Mr. McGregor is going to do about those pesky rabbits? What will Peter say to Flopsy, Mopsy and Cotton-tail the morning after his adventure? What will they say to Peter? What will Peter's mother tell him the next time he goes out to play?

For *The Paperbag Princess:* What will the dragon do when he wakes up? What will become of the prince? What is the princess going to do next?

For *Pinocchio:* How do you think Pinocchio will act now that he has turned into a real boy?

You can also prompt your child to make up a story about what happens next. Write down the story as she's telling it, even if it's only a few sentences long (see Chapter 9, Be a Writer). Sometimes, when you reread the original story, you will want to read your young author's "sequel" as well.

Don't stop here. Follow up on subjects that spark your child's interest and help her make connections to the real world. For example, after reading *The Elephant's Child*, you can read a nonfiction book about crocodiles or alligators, or look at a map of Africa and hunt for the places Kipling mentions in the story. Or you can go to the zoo!

Remember that too many stops and starts interrupt the flow of reading. Too few questions fail to provide enough active reading practice. Your child will help you find your way to the right balance.

2 What Does This Mean?

SKILL: BUILDING VOCABULARY

You and your child are reading happily along when—holy sesquipedalian!*—a strange new word appears like a giant log blocking the middle of the road.

If your young reader doesn't understand this word, he might get stuck or miss something really important. But Real Readers are not easily discouraged. They can usually figure out what a new word means because they know how to look around and find clues to meaning.

You can, of course, simply explain the new word and read on, and some-times this is exactly what you'll do. However, each encounter with a new word is a great opportunity to teach a valuable active reading skill: how to figure out a word's meaning by using *context clues*, hints that are often right under the reader's nose! Real Readers automatically look for context clues whenever they run into an unfamiliar word or phrase.

Using context clues is such a useful skill that books for young people are usually chock full of many different kinds of them. Sometimes, an illustration is the clue to meaning. Or maybe the author tells you what the strange word or phrase means right away. For example, you don't have to look very far to find the definition of *ba* and *ka* in this sentence from *Mummies Made in Egypt*, by Aliki: "Egyptians believed everyone had a *ba*, or soul, and a *ka*, an invisible twin of a person."

But sometimes you have to figure out what a word probably means by looking carefully at other words or phrases around it in the sentence or even in the paragraph. For instance, here's a passage from Roald Dahl's *James and the Giant Peach*:

> . . . *James could see a mass of tiny green things that looked like little stones or crystals, each one about the size of a grain of rice. They were extraordinarily beautiful, and there was a strange brightness about them, a sort of* luminous *quality that made them glow and sparkle in the most wonderful way.*

With a bit of prompting, a child who doesn't understand *luminous* can figure out from the clues *brightness*, *glow*, and *sparkle* that it most likely means something like *shining* or *shiny* or *full of light*. And think about this: Later on, when he comes across *illuminate*, he'll be better equipped to guess what this word means.

More advanced readers move on to look up unfamiliar words in the dictionary. Using a dictionary is another skill you will want to demonstrate to a young reader as soon as the books you are reading together seem to call for it.

For the beginning reader (and often for the more experienced reader, as well) it's a lot more fun, and gives the brain a better workout, to figure out the mystery word on his own. Even very young readers can learn to be on the lookout for context clues if you point the way every time you read together, every time you come up against a strange word.

Remember: Youngsters have a huge capacity for learning new words! All they need is encouragement and a bit of practice. It goes without saying that the bigger your child's vocabulary, the more able he is to comprehend what he's reading. So don't shy away from books with words you think may be too hard. You'll be surprised at the extent and complexity of vocabulary he will acquire.

* Did you guess? *Sesquipedalian* means "long and ponderous" or "a long word."

Finding Context Clues

Read aloud. If your child can read, take turns reading.

Be on the lookout for words your child may not know.

Do not stop when you first meet up with a new word. Read the entire sentence or paragraph (sometimes even the whole page) that contains the word.

Ask: Do you know this word? What do you think it means?

Point out context clues, words, or pictures that can help a child find the way to meaning.

Reinforce the new word by asking your child to remind you what it means when you see it again. If possible, use the new word in everyday conversation.

That's all there is to it! While interpreting context clues can get harder as your child moves on to more complicated reading material, the basic approach stays the same.

Readers who look for context clues learn to:

♦ Read attentively
♦ Make logical guesses
♦ Stretch their vocabularies
♦ Think creatively

Example #1

Even the simplest children's stories contain words that young children are meeting for the first time. Take *Goldilocks and the Three Bears.* When a hungry Goldilocks stumbles upon the bears' house, she finds three bowls of *porridge.*

Ask: Can you guess what *porridge* is?

Say: The story is giving us clues. *Porridge* is in a bowl. It's something to eat.

It can be hot; it can be cold; or it can be just right. Remember, it's breakfast time . . .

Praise the child who guesses "some kind of cereal" and ask him to name different kinds of hot cereal, for example oatmeal or Cream of Wheat.

OR

Say: Good thinking! (If your child suggests spaghetti, soup, or some other food.) Spaghetti or soup is hot, and eaten out of a bowl. *Porridge* is another kind of food. *Porridge* means hot cereal. Can you tell me the name of your favorite *porridge*?

Reinforce the new word. Next time you serve oatmeal, ask your child to pass the *porridge.*

Example #2

The Dr. Seuss classic *Horton Hatches the Egg* introduces Mayzie, a lazy bird, who can't be bothered to hang around waiting for her egg to hatch. She asks Horton, a trustworthy elephant, to sit on her nest while she takes a short break.

The elephant laughed.
"Why of all silly things!
I haven't feathers and I haven't
*   wings.*

*ME on your egg? Why, that
doesn't make sense . . .
Your egg is so small, ma'am, and
I'm so immense."*

Ask: Do you know what *immense* means? What do you think it means?

Praise the child who guesses what *immense* means. Ask him to explain how he figured it out.

OR

Say: Let's look at the picture. How big is the egg? How big is the elephant? Which is bigger, the egg or the elephant? Let's look at what Horton says ("Your egg is so small, ma'am, and I'm so *immense* . . ."). Do you think that Horton is trying to tell Mayzie he's much bigger than her egg? Do you think *immense* means big or small?

Reinforce the word. Call a big lollipop an *immense* lollipop, or an oversized book an *immense* book, for example. Think of other animals who are *immense*: dinosaurs, giraffes, King Kong! You can even think of *immense* people, like Arnold Schwarzenegger, Goliath, or the giant in *Jack in the Beanstalk*.

Example #3

William Steig's fanciful children's books make effective use of challenging words. In *Sylvester and the Magic Pebble*, a young donkey out on a stroll one rainy afternoon comes upon a shiny red pebble. As he is holding it in his hoof, Sylvester makes a wish that it would stop raining:

To his great surprise, the rain stopped. It didn't stop gradually as rains usually do. It ceased. The drops vanished on the way down, the clouds disappeared, and everything was dry, and the sun was shining as if the rain had never existed.

In all his young life, Sylvester had never had a wish gratified so quickly.

When you finish reading this passage, there are several words you may want to highlight.

Ask: What did the rain do when it *ceased*? What hints does the book give you? What does the book say happened to the rain? (It stopped.) Do you think *cease* is another word for "stop"?

Praise the child who comes up with the right answer.

OR

Reread the sentences before and after "It ceased." Help your child spot the missed clues.

Read on.

Ask: Do you know what *vanished* means? Is there another word nearby that might mean the same thing? (*Disappeared.*) What's another way to say *disappear*? (*Go away.*)

Praise a correct answer,

OR

Help your reader find the clues to the answer.

Read on.

Ask: What does it mean to say that Sylvester's wish was *gratified*? What did Sylvester wish for? (That it would stop raining.) Did it stop raining? (Yes.) Did Sylvester's wish come true? (Yes.) Then if his wish came true, what does that mean? (It means his wish was *gratified*: in other words, he got what he wanted.) Do you have a wish? What would happen if your wish were *gratified*?

Reinforce these new words whenever you can. You might tell your child to *cease* when you want him to stop. You can note that the chocolate chip cookies have *vanished*. You will surely have an occasion to tell him that not every wish he has can be *gratified*!

Example #4

Sundiata: Lion King of Mali, by David Wisniewski, is the legend of a famous warrior-prince who lived in a small West African kingdom in the eleventh century. Here is how the story opens:

Listen to me, children of the Bright Country, and hear the great deeds of ages past. The words I speak are those of my father and his father before him, pure and full of truth. For we are griots. Centuries of law and learning reside within our minds. Thus we serve kings with the wisdom of history, bringing to life the lessons of the past so that the future may flourish.

Ask: What are *griots* (pronounced GREE-ohs)? What clues does the beginning of the story give?

Reread the introduction, hunting for clues. For example: A *griot* speaks the words of his father and grandfather. A *griot* has knowledge of law and learning and history. A *griot* serves kings in some way.

Note that *griot* has several possible meanings: storyteller, historian, royal advisor, wise man or woman.

Reinforce the meaning of the new word every time it recurs in the story until you feel that your reader has mastered it.

Example #5

In "I Hear America Singing," a poem that will be enjoyed by older children, poet Walt Whitman celebrates the pride and pleasure workers take in their work.

I hear America singing, the varied
carols I hear,
Those of mechanics, each one
singing his as it should be
blithe and strong,
The carpenter singing his as he
measures his plank or beam,
The mason singing his as he
makes ready for work,
or leaves off work,
The boatman singing what
belongs to him in his boat,
the deckhand singing on the
steamboat deck,
The shoemaker singing as he sits
on his bench,
The hatter singing as he stands. . . .

The words in italics are some words that are:

Words your child may know already;

Words that he can figure out from context clues;

Words that may have to be looked up.

Ask: What do you think this poem is about?

Talk about the general subject of the poem, the pleasure of working at a job you enjoy and doing it well.

Identify words your child may not know (*mason*, for example) and look them up; words that are related to words your child may know (*varied*, for example—like various); words to figure out from context clues: *carols* (something you sing); *plank, beam* (something the carpenter measures); and *hatter* (coming right after *shoemaker*, this will be easy!).

Ask: What do you think *blithe* means? The poem hints that it has something to do with the way the carols, or songs, are sung. Look it up in a dictionary to confirm or correct your child's guess. When workers sing *blithely*, they are singing *merrily* or *cheerfully*.

Stretch vocabulary by linking new words to words your child knows. (For example, *mechanics*, *carpenters*, and *shoemakers* are names for different kinds of workers.)

Ask: How many other kinds of workers can you name? (Teachers, doctors, sanitation workers, salespeople, bakers, gardeners, and so forth.)

FOLLOW-UP

Every waking moment is a vocabulary opportunity for young children, who are able to acquire language quickly and in truly astonishing quantity. Think for a moment about all the words a three-year-old (even one who isn't an especially good talker) has learned to say and all the stuff he can understand!

Reading provides a setting and a structure for focusing on new words and for figuring out words we don't know. However, you can help build a child's vocabulary any time, not just when you are reading together.

Feature the word of the week. Post a juicy new word in a prominent place—on the refrigerator, for example. This will remind you both to use it all week long.

Play word games. Look for words—new words, familiar words, nonsense words—whenever you take your child shopping.

Nothing's easier to do at the supermarket. Let's say you find *crunch* on a box of cereal. Ask your child to come up with rhyming words: *munch, punch, bunch,* and *lunch* will do just fine. Or, if you're looking for *tuna fish,* you can take turns naming other kinds of fish: *bluefish, redfish, sardines, swordfish.* At the butcher's counter, play around with names of animals. What's another word for *chicken*? (*Hen, poultry, fowl, chick.*) What's another word for a *baby cow*? (*Calf.*) What's another word for a grown-up *lamb*? (*Sheep.*)

You can play games like these wherever you and your child go: in a toy store, at the bank, in a clothing shop, and, of course, at the library. Your child should be aware that the world is filled with an endless supply of wonderful words.

3 Tell the Difference

SKILL: IDENTIFYING DIFFERENT KINDS OF READING MATERIAL

Reading material comes in many, many forms. You can introduce your child to the varieties of written expression through stories, poems, fables, fairy tales, diaries, letters, cookbooks, and even plays, essays, and magazine articles.

A poem is not the same as a story, although some poems, such as epics and ballads, do tell stories. A story that someone made up (fiction) is not the same as a book about meteors or Mother Teresa (non-fiction). Non-fiction is an umbrella word for lots of different kinds of writing—biography and autobiography, reports, encyclopedias, newspapers, magazines, and more.

Can children tell the difference? Not at first. Most little kids think that Big Bird, Simba, Santa, and the tooth fairy are real and that stories about them are absolutely true. After all, nobody expects little kids to separate fact from fantasy. But this doesn't mean they can't learn how.

Come to think of it, it's surprising how rarely grown-ups talk to young children about what *kind* of stuff they are reading. And yet, aren't children born with the ability to tell things apart? Is there a toddler on earth who confuses broccoli with ice cream? Kids can certainly figure out which TV shows or videos they like and which ones they don't. Even a three-year-old will tell you that the cartoon channel is great, but that C-Span is *bore-ring*.

Why should we care whether a young child can tell poetry from prose, fiction from non-fiction, or a biography from an autobiography? Because the young reader who can recognize a variety of forms has learned to make distinctions and put things into categories. This ability will pay off by the middle grades, if not sooner, when your child is challenged to read lots of different types of books and do lots of different kinds of writing, as in "What I Did on My Summer Vacation." Making distinctions also will come in handy when a child is asked to do research and make critical judgments.

This may sound complicated, but it isn't. Every form of writing contains clues to its special category, clues grown-ups recognize readily but a young reader may not. Many poems for youngsters rhyme and often have very strong rhythm as well. ("I went to the animal fair / The birds and the beasts were there.") Fairy tales often begin "Once upon a time," or with some similar phrase that signals our emergence into a make-believe world of princes, princesses, witches, and wizards. Myths are traditional stories about how the world and nature came to be. Fables often feature talking animals and end with a lesson or a moral. Letters start "Dear Someone," and diaries start "Dear Diary." A cookbook has pages of recipes. A play is written in dialogue and is meant to be acted. You know all this. A new reader has to learn it.

When is the best time to alert your child that there are different types of reading material? As soon as she asks, "Did that really happen?" or, "Is this true?" Or as soon as she gets her first birthday card from Aunt Shirley. Or every time she sees you pick up a newspaper, a magazine, or a menu. These are golden opportunities to explain that there are many different kinds of things to read, to name them, and to show their similarities and differences.

This skill comes with a bonus: Teaching children to separate fact from fiction early on can help them distinguish between TV commercials and the shows they interrupt! The sooner your child learns to tell the difference between entertainment, education, and a sales pitch, the better.

Identifying Different Kinds of Reading Material

Talk about how we are constantly reading many different kinds of things (for example, newspapers, letters, magazines, catalogues, and e-mail).

Ask: Can you think of anything else we read? What kinds of things have we read today?

Each time you pick up something to read, spend a moment talking about what it is.

Say: This is a picture book, it has lots of pictures and no (or few) words, and it is fiction, a made-up story. This is a fairy tale, a fictional story about fantastic creatures and adventures. This is a biography, a true story about a real person. This is a poem. In this poem, the words at the end of the lines rhyme, or sound alike. This is an autobiography. The writer is telling us about her life in her own words. This is a non-fiction book. The writer is telling us something true about _____ (fill in the blank: cowboys, penguins, the stars).

Read aloud. If your child can read, take turns reading.

Readers who can identify different kinds of material learn to:

♦ Make distinctions
♦ Generalize
♦ Think critically
♦ Appreciate different literary forms

Example #1

"Before I Go to Sleep," by Thomas Hood, is a delightful poem, enchantingly illustrated by Maryjane Begin-Callanan. At the end of a summer day, a little boy is stretched out on his bed, dreaming about all the wonderful and strange animals he would like to be. Here is the first verse:

I think I'd be a glossy cat
A little plump, but not too fat.
I'd never touch a bird or mouse
I'm much too busy round the
*   house.*

He goes on to dream about being a fierce and hungry hound, a crocodile, a mountain goat, a polar bear, a wise old frog, a lion, a tall giraffe, a clever fox, a chimpanzee, and a snake with scales of gold. This is the way the poem ends:

But then before I really know
Just what I'd be or where I'd go
My bed becomes so wide and deep
And all my thoughts are fast
*   asleep.*

Ask: How do we know this is a poem? (Because it rhymes.)

Explain that rhymes are words that sound alike. (Later you can explain that poems do not have to rhyme, such as the Walt Whitman poem in Chapter 2.)

Ask: Can you think of another poem that rhymes? (Mother Goose rhymes, for example.) Can you think of a word that rhymes with blue? (Shoe, true, you, is two, who, moo, Winnie the Pooh.)

Say: Let's see if we can make up another verse to this poem. Begin: "I think I'd be a _____." (For example, "I think I'd be a big, red bird / Who sings but never says a word . . .")

Add a new verse each time you read the poem.

When you think your child is ready:

Ask her to make up her own poem. She can decide whether it should rhyme or not.

Write down your child's verses and reread them next time you open a book of poetry.

Example #2

The title of *The Legend of Sleepy Hollow* lets the reader know right away that this is fiction, a story someone made up long ago that has been passed down over the years. Many writers have adapted and many artists have illustrated this Washington Irving classic. One of the most charming versions for children is retold and illustrated by Will Moses.

In the story, which is set in a valley called Sleepy Hollow, the townspeople talk about a ghost, a horseman without a head. This restless horseman rides through the countryside in search of his head, and when the sun comes up he returns to the cemetery where he was buried without it.

One night, Ichabod Crane, a skinny schoolmaster with a big imagination, is chased by a hideous figure he believes to be the Headless Horseman. What Ichabod does not know (but we do) is that the horseman is really a young man named Brom Bones. The horrible head, which Ichabod sees perched on the horseman's saddle, is nothing but a pumpkin. Brom is playing a practical joke on Ichabod, who has been courting the young beauty whom Brom is also pursuing. The timid schoolmaster is so terrified by the Headless Horseman that he is literally frightened out of town—which leaves the way clear for Brom to marry his sweetheart, who was never interested in Ichabod in the first place.

Ask: What is a legend? Do you think this really happened? (It might have, but the writer wasn't there when it happened, so he had to make up the story.) Do you think something like this could happen? (Yes, but that doesn't mean it's true.)

Explain that made-up stories are called fiction. The writer of fiction can make up anything he wants because he is free to use his imagination.

Talk about other fiction you have read together. (At this point, most of the books you've read to your young reader probably *are* fiction.)

Predict what happens to Ichabod after he leaves Sleepy Hollow. What happens to Brom Bones and his sweetheart? Does the Headless Horseman ever ride again?

Example #3

There are plenty of first-rate non-fiction books for children, many of them with outstanding illustrations or photographs. There's absolutely no reason to wait until your child is older to introduce non-fiction into reading time. If you know, for example, that your son or daughter likes Barney, you can read a simple book about real dinosaurs after you finish a book about Barney.

Next, try a bit of a stretch. Little dinosaur-lovers will also be wild about *Wild and Woolly Mammoths*, written and illustrated by Aliki, which is part of a Let's Read and Find Out series on a wide variety of subjects likely to be of interest to young readers. This book is chock full of information on these beasts, who lived eons ago during the last Ice Age, long after the dinosaurs disappeared, and who grew heavy coats of hair to protect them from the cold.

In this little book, your young reader will learn how one mammoth's body came to be encased in ice so that scientists could find it and study it 10,000 years later. She will also learn that there were much bigger imperial mammoths who lived 3 million years ago who were not woolly because they lived in warm climates.

Ask: Do you think there were ever such animals as woolly mammoths? How can we find out? (If you are lucky enough to be near a museum of natural history, you may have seen a model of one. Or, look up *mammoth* in the encyclopedia.)

On a map or globe, find the places where woolly mammoths lived: Europe, China, Siberia, and Alaska. Are these real places?

Talk about non-fiction, material that is not invented or made up.

Ask: Have we read other books about real things and real people? What real things and real people were these books about?

Name something or someone in the real world and tell what you know (for example, Grandma, an astronaut, turtles).

Example #4

The *Fables* of Aesop are very familiar, although many people don't know that Aesop was a Greek slave who lived in the sixth century B.C. As you will recall, fables usually feature talking animals and pay off with a moral or lesson. The most famous of these include "The Tortoise and the Hare" and "The Boy Who Cried Wolf."

There are many individual versions of the best known of Aesop's fables; several collections of the complete fables are also in print. This example, "The Town Mouse and the Country Mouse," is drawn from Barnes and Noble's reprint of the classic *Aesop for Children*, illustrated by Milo Winter.

A town mouse takes a trip to the country to visit her cousin. But the town mouse does not think much of the country mouse's simple home and plain food. She urges the country mouse to come to the town, where mice live in the lap of luxury.

When the country mouse pays a visit to town, she is at first extremely impressed. The town mouse lives in a mansion and dines on rich foods. But every time the two cousins try to nibble on the remains of a splendid dinner, they are frightened away from the table, first by a cat, then by servants, then by a dog. Terrified, the country mouse decides to go back to her humble cottage in the fields. Far better, says she, to be poor and safe than to be rich and always afraid.

Ask: Do you think this really happened? Can mice really talk? Is this fiction or non-fiction? Is it a poem? (In some retellings, it may be!)

Explain that a fable is a tale that uses animals as characters and teaches an important lesson.

Ask: Can you think of any other fables we have read?

Think up a story about an animal who talks and acts like a person. Does your story end with a lesson?

Ask: Is *The Tale of Peter Rabbit*, by Beatrix Potter, a fable? (Yes.) Why? (It features animals that talk and act like people and ends with a lesson: Always listen to your mother.)

Example #5

Teammates, by Peter Golenbock, is a fine biography for younger readers. In this instance, we have a book about not one but two people, the famous ballplayers Jackie Robinson and Pee Wee Reese.

This book is set in the 1940s when, in addition to suffering many other forms of racial discrimination, black people were not welcome in the majors and played baseball in their own leagues, the Negro Leagues.

Branch Rickey, the white general manager of the Brooklyn Dodgers, sought out Robinson, a star player from the Negro Leagues who was brave and tough. Robinson knew that if he succeeded in a major ballclub, he would pave the way for other black players. Even though he was treated very roughly by white players and fans, and especially by the men on his team who came from the South, Robinson stayed calm. He kept his focus on the game and played outstandingly.

One white player, Dodger shortstop Pee Wee Reese, was not like the others. He felt that a person should be judged on how well he played, not on the color of his skin, and he wouldn't sign a petition to throw Robinson off the team. One afternoon, when Pee Wee heard white fans yelling abuse at Jackie at a ballpark near Pee Wee's hometown, he decided to take a stand. He walked to where Jackie was playing first base and, in front of everyone, put his arm around Jackie and said, "This man is my teammate."

Ask: Do you think this really happened?

Talk about *biography*, the story of somebody's life. Once a reader gets the idea, it's an easy jump to *autobiography*, a book that someone writes about his own life in his own words.

Ask: Have we read any other biographies or autobiographies?

Find other books regarding people your young reader would like to know more about in your library or bookstore.

Be the biographer, in a few words, of someone you know. (José was born in Puerto Rico and lived there until he was six.)

Be an autobiographer and tell your own story in your own words. (I was born in Sandusky, Ohio, and have lived here all my life.)

FOLLOW-UP

Once your young reader has collected a whole bunch of books, encourage her to organize them by category. She can separate the fiction from the non-fiction and put each group in a separate place. Then she can put biographies (Jackie Robinson) and books about nature (woolly mammoths) on one side of the shelf, and all the fiction (*The Legend of Sleepy Hollow*) on the other side. Poetry can have its own special place.

When you visit the library, point out that librarians organize their books in very much the same way. The goal is to communicate these ideas:

- ◆ There are different kinds of books to read
- ◆ They have different names
- ◆ We can learn to tell them apart
- ◆ We can generalize (put books into categories)

This may seem like no big deal, but it's an important concept, and because it seems so obvious, many parents neglect to mention it to their young children.

4 Say It in Your Own Words

SKILL: RESTATING

Somebody's giving you directions, instructions, explanations, or predictions. You want to be sure you understand what you've been told and, what's more, that you remember it. What do you do? You repeat it in your own words, trying to be sure not to leave out anything important. You restate.

Real Readers automatically put things into their own words. They know how to restate what they read. They keep the sequence of events in the right order. They know which details to keep in mind and which to put aside.

Being able to present a story or article in your own words is an enormously useful reading and study skill. When a young reader can restate what he's read, he strengthens his memory, he clarifies what he understands, and he pinpoints what he doesn't. These are important steps toward mastery of any subject.

When restating isn't simple, Real Readers reread. They look up unfamiliar words. They hunt for clues they may have missed. Sometimes they discover that they had trouble understanding because the writer wasn't clear in the first place!

If your young reader restates the story to you when he gets to the end, both of you will have a good idea of how much he has understood and how much he hasn't. Perhaps he's overlooked a small but meaningful point. For instance, the child who reads "The Boy Who Cried Wolf" must catch the fact that the boy cried "wolf" not just once but *many times* before the townspeople ignored his calls for help. If the reader misses this fact, he cannot comprehend the point of the story: If you keep telling lies, nobody's going to believe you even when you are telling the truth.

Athletes often "play up" by seeking opponents who are just a bit better than they are. This is a way to challenge themselves and improve. As beginning readers become more advanced readers, you should test their abilities by asking them to read up and restate passages from increasingly challenging books. How do you know when your child is ready to do

this? If you ask him to restate and he can, consistently, it's time.

Putting the Story in Your Own Words

How soon does it make sense to start asking a young reader to retell a story or part of a story? It all depends on the reader's verbal skills and comprehension level and on how hard the material is. A very young child can give you a pretty good idea of what is going on in *The Three Little Pigs*, probably by partially acting it out. But the same child, who may have watched the film *Babe* more times than you care to think about, won't be able to tell you anything coherent about it for quite some time.

Sometimes, of course, a kid just wants a parent to read while he just sits quietly and listens. There's nothing wrong with this! But there's a lot right with trying to get a young reader actively engaged. Saying to your child, "Now it's *your* turn to tell me the story," is a natural way to get going.

Read aloud. If your child can read, take turns reading.

Stop occasionally (but not too often; you don't want to disrupt the flow of reading) to ask what's going on in the story. If your child is missing the point, don't worry. Things often clear up right on the next page.

Say: Let's read on a little. We can always go back if we don't understand what's going on.

OR

Say: Let's read that part again. Let's figure out what that word means. Did that happen before or after this happened?

OR

If the reader can restate the story,

Say: Good job! You really got it!

If he makes a mistake, like: misunderstanding a key word, or getting the sequence of events confused, or leaving out something really important,

Prompt him to find the clues that point the way to the answer.

Readers who practice restating learn to:

- Pick out the most important points
- Identify something they may have missed
- Keep things in the proper order
- Remember what they have read

Example #1

Start with something easy. Does your child ever get a letter? Children love to get mail! You can easily use letters (or e-mail, if you've got it) as a springboard for restating. You can ask friends and relatives to write to your child, or you can write a letter or postcard yourself. When you think of it, incorporate some new vocabulary words your child has learned.

Read the letter together.

Figure out unfamiliar words.

Prompt your child to tell somebody else (to restate) what is in the letter. Make sure he conveys the most important things the writer had to say.

Reinforce: Ask your child to dictate or write a reply. (See Chapter 9, "Be A Writer.")

Example #2

The Little Red Hen is a good little story for young readers to retell. It's simple. It's logical. Because each step in the story is equally important to the outcome, beginners don't have to pick and choose what's relevant, what they have to leave in, and what they can leave out. As a bonus, the story ends with a clever lesson, presented with a light touch.

There are many versions of this tale, but the basics are always the same. The little red hen finds a grain of wheat on the ground. She goes to her three friends, the duck, the cat, and the dog. She asks, "Who will help plant the wheat?" One by one, her friends refuse, each one saying, "Not I." So the little red hen does it herself.

And so it goes, on through the cutting of the wheat and the threshing (good vocabulary word!), and the taking of the wheat to the mill to have it ground (another!) into flour, until it's time to make the flour into bread. But when she asks who will help her eat the bread, the little red hen's three friends line right up for a slice. "Oh, no, you won't!" says the little red hen, and she shares the bread with her own three chicks.

Read the whole story, stopping, if necessary, to clarify any unfamiliar words.

Say: Now, you tell the story of the little red hen.

If your reader has difficulty (and he well may, after only one reading),

Say: Let's read the story again. Now can you tell me the story?

If the story comes out with all five steps (planting, cutting, threshing, grinding, and baking) in order,

Say: Good for you! You really understand this story.

If your child omits a step or gets mixed up,

Say: Let's read the story one more time.

Ask: What is the first thing that happens? What does the little red hen do first? What happens next?

Can the wheat grow without being planted in the ground?

Can the little red hen bake the bread before the wheat is ground into flour? Can you think of anything we do, step by step? (Following a recipe is a good example, or even getting dressed. After all, you don't put on your shoes before you put on your socks.)

Or, if your child is not ready to retell the story, move on and try again after you have reread the story a few times. Remember: This is not a test. Retelling should be fun, not a chore.

Example #3

Robert McCloskey's classic *Make Way for Ducklings* begins in the big city of Boston, where Mr. and Mrs. Mallard are looking for a pleasant, quiet place to hatch their ducklings.

After much thought, they choose a spot on a bank of a river. Every day they swim to the other side, where a friendly police officer named Michael feeds them peanuts.

In due time, eight ducklings hatch. While Mr. Mallard scouts for a permanent home, Mrs. Mallard teaches the little ducks to swim and dive, to walk behind her in a line, and to come when they are called. So she feels confident when she decides to gather up her children and journey to meet Mr. Mallard, who has found the perfect spot, a little island in the middle of a pond in the middle of the Public Garden in the middle of the city.

But on the way to their new home, Mrs. Mallard and her ducklings come to a highway. No matter how hard they all quack, the speeding cars do not stop to let them cross. Finally, Officer Michael hears them quacking and comes running. "He planted himself in the center of the road, raised one hand to stop the traffic, and than beckoned with the other, the way policemen do, for Mrs. Mallard to cross over." As soon as they go by, Michael calls ahead to let other police officers know that a family of ducks is coming!

As the police hold back the traffic, Mrs. Mallard and her eight ducklings make their way safely through the city streets and on into the Public Garden, where Mr. Mallard is waiting for them. They settle in happily on the little island, and it turns out that they have picked a fine place to raise a family.

Read the whole story, stopping, if necessary, to work out the meaning of words like *horrid* (this is how Mrs. Mallard describes a bicycle) and *opposite bank* (the shore on the other side of the river).

Say: Now you tell the story. Can you try to make it shorter than the story we just read? You can leave things out that you don't think I need to know.

Prompt your child to express the general ideas in a way that makes sense. Your goal is to have a reader grasp the general sequence of events and to *condense* the story by leaving out unnecessary details.

Here's one way to retell the story: First, the Mallards are looking for a good, safe place to raise a family. Second, Mrs. Mallard has a number of ducklings and teaches them how to behave. Third, Mr. Mallard goes on ahead to their new home and waits for them. Fourth, Mrs. Mallard sets out with all the ducklings to meet him. Fifth, the ducks' friend, a police officer, helps them to get to

their destination safely. And sixth, they all live happily ever after in their new home.

If your child comes up with a more detailed retelling, you might:

Say: Let's think about what's *most* important in this story. Is the number of ducklings important? (Not really.) Are the names of the ducklings important? (No.) Is the Mallards' reason for wanting a home important? (Yes.) Is the fact that a police officer is the ducks' friend important? (Yes.) Is the name of the street they cross important? (Nope.) Is Officer Mike's call ahead to the other police officers important? (Yup.)

Praise the reader who can retell *Make Way for Ducklings* in a short and logical way.

If he omits something important, such as the fact that the duck family is looking for a home, or gets the order confused, such as reuniting

Mr. and Mrs. Mallard *before* Officer Mike stops the traffic,

Ask: Why do Mr. and Mrs. Mallard want to find a home? Who is the ducks' friend? Where does Mr. Mallard go after the ducklings are born? How does the family get back together? When does the family get back together?

Example #4

Biography provides a fine opportunity for practicing this skill because biography has a logical shape: It begins with the beginning of a person's life and ends at the end. A thoughtful biography for somewhat more advanced readers is *Rachel Carson* by William Accorsi.

Right on the first page, the author notifies the reader, "This is the story of a child who loved nature." We read on about the biologist's Pennsylvania childhood, how she started to write her own stories, and about her education. After finishing school, she went to work for the government in the Bureau of Fisheries and wrote two books about the oceans. One, *The Sea Around Us*, made her very well-known.

In *Rachel Carson*, an aunt wrote to Rachel, wondering why she was finding so many dead birds in her neighborhood. Rachel realized that the chemicals farmers were using to kill weeds and insects were killing other plants and animals as well. She wrote a book called *Silent Spring* to bring this problem to everyone's attention.

Thanks to Rachel Carson, people began to think about ways to protect the environment. Her influence continues to this day, even though her book was written many decades ago.

Before you read, remind your child that a biography is the true story of somebody's life.

Say: Now that you have read this biography, what do you know about Rachel Carson?

Prompt the reader to begin with Rachel's childhood; mention her schooling; include her first job; remember the subject of her successful book (and the title, for extra points!); talk about her concern for the environment.

Reinforce: Find other biology books. Find other biographies. Find out the year Rachel Carson died. (The date is not in this book!)

Example #5

A lovely Polynesian myth is beautifully retold by Virginia Hamilton in her Newbery Award–winning *In the Beginning: Creation Stories from Around the World*.

According to the Society Islanders of Polynesia, the ancient god Ta-aroa lived in an egg-shaped shell that floated in space for a long, long time. One day, Ta-aroa emerged from the egg and, finding himself all alone in the middle of nothingness, made a companion-god named Tu. Together they created the universe and filled it with land, plants and animals, gods like themselves and, finally, the first man, Ti-i, and Hina, his good-hearted wife.

Ti-i was a cruel man who used magic to stir up trouble in the world. Soon his mischief made Ta-aroa and Tu so angry that they cursed the moon, the stars, the sea, the trees, and even the people who lived on earth. Fortunately, Hina, who was half-goddess, saved nature from destruction. But she could do nothing to prevent men and women from losing eternal life.

Before you read, tell or remind your listener of the story of Genesis: God created the world in six days and made Eve from Adam's rib, Eve offered Adam fruit from a tree God had forbidden them to touch, and Adam and Eve were sent away from the Garden of Eden because they had defied God's command. If your reader already knows the story, ask him to tell it to you.

Explain that myths are traditional stories about the world and nature that come down to us from people who lived thousands of years ago. A *creation myth* accounts for the beginnings of our world and all its living creatures. Different people in different lands tell different stories about how the world began.

Read the story of Ta-aroa together.

Ask your child to tell you what a myth is and then to retell the myth of Ta-aroa.

Focus on the similarities and differences between the story of Ta-aroa and the story of Genesis. For example: Both stories say there was nothingness in the world in the very beginning. Ta-aroa made Tu help him create the universe; God did it alone. The Polynesians believed that because of the first man's cruelty, humans lost eternal life; the Bible says that because of the first woman's disobedience, humans had to leave Paradise.

Read other creation stories in Hamilton's book and in collections of Greek and Roman mythology. Ask your child to tell them back to you or someone else in the family. Again, compare and contrast these versions of the world's beginning.

FOLLOW-UP

Have regular storytelling times when you put all books aside and take turns retelling favorite stories. This is a constructive way to pass time when you're in the car or waiting to see the dentist or standing in line at the checkout counter.

Seize other opportunities to prompt your child to put a story in his own words. The average day is full of possibilities: a favorite movie or video, a song, a poem, a family trip, a conversation with a friend, a visit to Grandma and Grandpa, or the story of a special holiday.

5 See Through Someone Else's Eyes

SKIILL: BECOMING AWARE OF POINT OF VIEW

Children naturally think they're the center of the universe no matter how hard we try to make them see things from other people's point of view. "How would *you* feel if your brother bopped *you* on the head?" we ask. Or, "Do you suppose the puppy likes it when you pull its ears?" Or, "Aunt Irene will be sad if you don't thank her for your present!"

The idea that there can be more than one way of looking at things may be a little slippery at first for a young child. However, this is a concept worth introducing early on, for two big reasons. First, the more a child can see through somebody else's eyes, the more she will be able to appreciate the experiences and emotions all people have in common, and to respect their differences as well. Second, she will come to understand a concept that squabbling siblings usually have a hard time learning—there is *always* more than one side to every story.

Real Readers always consider point of view when they read. They know that our understanding of life expands and deepens when we try to see the world as others see it. They also understand that every author, whether writing a novel or a political speech, is offering his interpretation of events and trying to convince us that his is the real story. However, just because something's in print doesn't mean it's true or that we have to believe it 100 percent. A lot depends on who is doing the telling.

Since stories, poems, articles, biographies, and even nursery rhymes were all written by Somebody, they all represent Somebody's point of view. Sometimes a book lets us know exactly through whose eyes we are being asked to look. Sometimes we have to figure out for ourselves whose viewpoint is being expressed and whether we should trust the teller.

When a person writes about his own life, it's obvious who's talking. "I did this," the writer says. "I said that." Autobiography (the writer's own story of his own life) will surely differ from biography (a life story filtered through the point of view of somebody else). The autobiographer may want to gloss over or leave out a lot of nasty details that the biographer can't wait to reveal.

Fiction is more complicated. Even though the writer may seem to be an objective observer and reporter, he is in fact presenting a story with a particular slant. For example, in the fairy tale *Cinderella*, the Brothers Grimm are definitely on Cinderella's side. Imagine how different the story would be if the stepmother were telling it. She might well say: "That sneaky Cinderella! She made up this totally ridiculous story about a fairy godmother, crashed the ball, and stole the prince right out from under my beautiful daughters' noses!" If, on the other hand, the prince were telling the tale, he would probably start with how his parents nagged him to get married. If you think about it, doesn't it seem pretty clear that *Cinderella* is told from Cinderella's point of view?

The skill of recognizing point of view comes increasingly into play as young readers mature. When they read nonfiction, particularly news articles and editorials, they must be able to separate the facts from the writer's opinion. To appreciate literature, they must be able to tune in to the motivations and perspectives of the various characters.

It takes time to teach children to grasp the subtleties of point of view, but you can pave the way by gently getting them used to the idea right off the bat. As soon as you feel your young reader is ready, ask: *Who is telling this story? How do you know? Are there other ways to look at this story?* Real Readers, active readers involved in a give-and-take with what they read, always want to know.

Identifying Point of View

Talk about the idea of point of view and how, depending upon who is doing the looking, it is possible to look at things in many different ways.

Check the title or opening words to see if you can spot a clue to who's telling the story. "I'm a little teapot," for example, tells you immediately who is speaking.

Read aloud. If your child can read, take turns reading.

Ask: Whose side do you think the author is on? (For example, are we supposed to be on Jack's side or on the side of the giant at the top of the beanstalk? Are we on the side of the three little pigs or on the side of the wolf? You might observe that when a character is called the big bad wolf, it's pretty clear the writer isn't on his side!)

Explore the different points of view of the characters in the story. The seven dwarfs in Walt Disney's popular version of *Snow White* are good examples because it is clear that they see the world in different ways: grumpily, happily, dope-ily, bashfully, sleepily, sneeze-ily. (You figure out how Doc feels.)

Readers who practice identifying point of view learn to:

- Be aware of who is telling a story
- Understand the different perspectives of different characters
- Develop empathy
- Think critically

Example #1

More than a few books deliberately play around with point of view. One of the most satisfying is *The True Story of the 3 Little Pigs! by A. Wolf* (as told to Jon Scieszka).

The fact that it is Mr. Wolf who is writing this book should tell your young reader something! The very first words signal what is going on here: Everybody, he says, thinks they know the story of the three little pigs; but nobody knows the real story because nobody has heard *his* side.

According to Alexander T. Wolf, he has been getting a bad rap, and all because he had "a terrible sneezing cold" and ran out of sugar while trying to make a birthday cake for his dear old granny. The first neighbor from whom he tried to borrow sugar was a little pig who lived in a straw house.

You can predict what happened. Wolf had to sneeze, and as he huffed and puffed, the straw house came down, killing the first little pig. No point letting a good meal go to waste, so Wolf ate the little pig up. Then he moved on to the next house, a house made of sticks, which was the house of the first little pig's brother. Another sneeze, another pile of rubble, another dead pig, a second helping.

The third little pig, notes A. Wolf, was "the brains of the family," for his house was made of bricks. This pig refused to open his door and this made Wolf so angry that he huffed and puffed until the cops came and took him away. So this story, it turns out, is being written from jail!

Ask: Who is telling this story? (the big—is he *really* bad?—wolf) Why? (He wants to tell the true story; he wants to make himself look good; he wants to get out of jail, etc.)

Pretend that you are the third little pig and explain to the police what happened to your brothers. Was Mr. Wolf really trying to borrow a cup of sugar? Why wouldn't you open your door and let him in?

Now pretend that you are a police officer describing what you found when you got to the third little pig's house.

Discuss: Whose story do you believe, the third little pig's or the wolf's? Why?

Example #2

In *The Escape of Marvin the Ape* by Caralyn and Mark Buehner, Marvin, a large, friendly ape, runs away from the zoo and roams around the city.

The story begins, "It was feeding time, and when the zookeeper wasn't looking, Marvin slipped out." He goes out for lunch, just like a person (he orders the Jungle Fruit Platter), and the waiter talks to him just as if he were a person, not an ape. He goes to the park, to the museum, to the movies, to a ball game, and for a ride on the ferry. Even though you don't usually see an ape in any of these places, Marvin fits right in, and nobody pays any attention to him. He is so content with his new life that he just keeps on going. At the end of the book, Helvetica the hippopotamus seizes the opportunity when the zookeeper's back is turned, and she dashes out to freedom.

Look at the cover illustration. (There's Marvin, peering out from behind the bars of his cage.)

Say: The title of this book is *The Escape of Marvin the Ape.*

Ask: Who is this on the cover? Does he look happy or sad? Why? If you were caged up in a zoo, how would you feel? What do you think Marvin is planning to do?

Talk about who is telling us about Marvin's adventures.

Ask: Is it Marvin who is speaking? (No.) How do you know? (He doesn't say "I.") Is the zookeeper telling the story? (No, because the zookeeper stays at the zoo while Marvin is gallivanting around the city.) Is it any of the people who see Marvin? (No, we don't hear from any of them.) Could it be Helvetica? (No, because she's still in the zoo until the end of the story.)

So who is telling this story? (Point out the names of the authors on the cover.) The idea here is to work your way to the point where the child understands that somebody who is not *in* the story is telling Marvin's story, and that this somebody is on Marvin's side.

Now pretend you are Marvin. How do you feel to be out in the world? What are you going to do? Where are you going to sleep? Do you plan to go back to the zoo?

Pretend you are the waiter or any of the other people who see Marvin. What would you do when you saw him? Would you want to make friends? Would you call a policeman to take him back to the zoo?

Pretend you are Helvetica. How did you feel when Marvin escaped? What are your plans?

Pretend you are the zookeeper. What did you think when Marvin disappeared? What did you do when Helvetica ran away, too?

Example #3

In Hans Christian Andersen's *Thumbelina*, a woman who desperately wants to have a child finds a tiny little girl in a flower and names her "Thumbelina" because the child is even smaller than the woman's thumb. (*Thumbelina* appears in all collections of Andersen fairy tales and in many stand-alone books. A particularly beautiful version is the one retold by Amy Ehrlich and illustrated by Susan Jeffers.)

While Thumbelina is wonderful in every way, she does not get any bigger. She sleeps under a rose-petal blanket in a cradle made from a walnut shell. Throughout the story, even though befriended by many tiny creatures, Thumbelina is often in danger because she is so very small.

Just at the moment when she feels she has no choice but to marry a mole whom she does not love, a swallow offers her a ride to a place where it is always summer. There, inside a flower, Thumbelina finds a prince who is exactly her size. He explains that he is king of the flower people and he asks Thumbelina to be his queen.

Look at the cover illustration and compare Thumbelina's size to her surroundings—or to your thumb!

Ask: Is Thumbelina a good name? Who is telling this story? (Hans Christian Andersen, Denmark's most famous writer and creator of other stories your child probably knows, like *The Ugly Duckling* and *The Little Mermaid.*) Is it possible for a real person to be as tiny as Thumbelina? Is this story fiction or nonfiction?

Pretend you are as little as Thumbelina.

Ask: How would you feel if you were much, much smaller than everyone else? What would you eat? How could you get around? Would it be better to be a giant? Have you ever read a story about a giant? (*Jack and the Beanstalk*, for example.)

Compare how a giant sees the world with how Thumbelina sees the world. For example, Thumbelina sleeps in a walnut shell. Can a giant sleep in a walnut shell? What would Thumbelina have for dinner? Would that be enough to satisfy a giant?

Ask: Do you know of any other little creatures? (Elves and fairies, for instance, or earthworms and ants.) Do you know of any other giant creatures? (Genies, Frankenstein, dinosaurs, and whales.) How do you think the world looks to them?

Example #4

Seek out books clearly intended to convey the feelings, thoughts, and experiences of others. In Patricia MacLachlan's *Through Grandpa's Eyes*, a book for older readers, young John tells how his grandfather, who is blind, has his own way of seeing.

At Grandpa's urging, John closes his eyes and can hear Nana, his grandmother, downstairs in the kitchen making breakfast. Grandpa prompts John to smell the eggs frying and the buttered toast.

Throughout the day, John and Grandpa do many things that help the boy understand his grandfather's way of "seeing." They play the cello and feel the south wind, and Grandpa identifies a bird by its song. Grandpa reads to Nana and John from a Braille book. When bedtime comes, Grandpa tucks John in and pulls the light chain to turn out the light. But, because the light is already off, he turns it on instead. This makes John smile.

Talk about the title.

Ask: What does it mean to see through someone else's eyes? What are the different ways Grandpa "sees" in this story? (He sees through his senses of hearing, smell, taste, and touch.) What kinds of things do you know other than by looking at them? (For example, you might know a dog is soft and furry by petting it, or that a glass has orange juice in it by smelling it.) What if you could not see? Would you be sad? Would you still be able to do many things? Does Grandpa seem sad? (No, he does not.) How does Nana help him? How would you help a person who cannot see? How does Grandpa feel about a visit from John? (They have a grand time together.)

Example #5

On the very first page of *Alexander and the Terrible, Horrible, No Good, Very Bad Day* by Judith Viorst,

Alexander tells us he is not a happy boy. He has hardly gotten out of bed and he has a list of complaints: he woke up with gum in his hair (after sleeping with gum in his mouth); he fell over a skateboard that he had left by the side of his bed; he dropped his sweater into a sink full of water. In Alexander's opinion, things are only going to get worse.

From the book's title, along with the tone of Alexander's voice and the illustrations by Ray Cruz, we know right away that Alexander thinks this might just be the rottenest day he has every had. He tells us about all the other disgusting things that happened, including the fact that there were lima beans for dinner and he hates limas, and there was kissing on TV and he hates kissing. He says he's going to move to Australia. However, his mom says that little boys sometimes have terrible days in Australia, too.

Although Alexander himself is speaking and the story represents Alexander's point of view, the writer signals in many ways that Alexander is simply dealing with everyday stuff, nothing that serious. After all, a kissing scene on TV isn't enough to ruin your life, and moving to Australia isn't a realistic option for a young boy.

Look at the cover. (It's a little boy clutching a pillow and looking very grumpy.)

Ask: Who do you think this boy is? Can you tell how he's feeling from the way he looks?

Read on.

Ask: Who is telling this story? (It's Alexander himself.) Why do you think he is telling us about his bad day? (He wants to complain, and he wants us to feel sorry for him.) Have you ever had a really bad day? If so, what went wrong? Would the story be different if Alexander's mother told it? How would she tell it? What if one of Alexander's brothers—Anthony or Nick—told about the same day? Would he tell the same story? Does this story make you feel sorry for Alexander? Was anything that happened during the day really so terrible? Do you think he's really going to move to Australia?

FOLLOW-UP

Turn familiar stories upside down by retelling them from other points of view. For example, if the giant were writing the story of Jack, he'd talk about the ruthless boy who climbed the giant's private beanstalk, invaded his home, and then stole the affections of his wife and his gold!

Make up little plays based on your children's favorite stories. Ask them to pretend to be different characters, and then to switch roles. Or ask one child to be one character, and then another. You can start with the seven dwarfs in Walt Disney's version of *Snow White.* Then try the ugly duckling, who just didn't fit in. How does the duckling feel?

Ask your child to pretend to be an animal, a thing, a flower—anything that's not human. Play along. If she's a puppy, pet her and throw her something to fetch. If she's a flower, pick and sniff her. If she's a fire engine, it's your turn to figure out what to do.

Look for versions of classic stories that have contrasting points of view. For example, in "The Tale of Aladdin and the Wonderful Lamp," the characters have different opinions about Aladdin. To his father, he's a lazy rascal; to his mother, a beloved son; to the magician, a foolish boy; to the sultan's daughter, a brave and worthy suitor. What does your young reader think of Aladdin? Why?

6 Read Between the Lines

SKILL: DRAWING INFERENCES

Imagine: You've just arrived at grandmother's cottage in the woods. You find your way to the room where Granny lies abed in her nightie. As you get closer, you notice that her ears and eyes are unusually large, her arms are strangely hairy, and her mouth is alarmingly wide and full of long, sharp teeth. What would you think?

Of course you'd conclude that all these clues spell W-O-L-F! But Little Red Riding Hood didn't get the picture until it was too late and the beast had gobbled her up—although, luckily for her, a passing hunter came to the rescue.

What Little Red clearly lacked was the ability to read between the lines, a reading skill that experts call *drawing inferences*. Like good detectives, Real Readers use clues in the story to discover something the writer does not say directly.

The whole point of reading, after all, is to understand all that the writer is trying to tell you. Sometimes, writers provide every single bit of information you need to know. However, many times, in fiction and poetry especially, they give you a hint here and there and

expect you to put two and two together! Real Readers, who know how to read between the lines, can go beyond the facts on the page to see deeper meanings in the story and get much more out of what they're reading.

Zillions of children's stories, from fables to fairy tales to poems, expect young readers to make all kinds of inferences. For example, the story of *Hansel and Gretel* doesn't tell us how the children felt about the stepmother who left them to die in the forest, but your child can easily infer what their feelings are and how he would react in the same situation. Or, he can apply similar powers of deduction to figure out the underlying message of *The Little Engine that Could*: if you try really hard to do something, you can succeed.

As they grow, our children will increasingly rely upon their ability to read between the lines, especially when they encounter more complex kinds of writing, such as poetry. This is a skill that children must master in order to succeed on standardized comprehension tests, which frequently contain questions requiring inference from a given paragraph or excerpt.

Reading between the lines is something competent grown-up readers do without even thinking about it. Next time you read a newspaper or a book, be alert to the many times that the writer expects you to read between the lines. The more you realize how often you use this skill, the easier it will be for you to spot opportunities in children's stories and poems for a young reader to do the same.

Making Inferences

The best children's stories can be read on many levels. Children at different stages of reading development and maturity find their way to different levels of meaning by using inference. Of course, a lot depends on how much reading experience they have.

Start with something simple. Pictures as well as words can serve as clues to meaning. For example, in Munro Leaf's *The Story of Ferdinand Bull*, the cover illustration shows a bull sniffing a flower. You can infer a lot about Ferdinand's gentle nature from this image.

Read aloud. Or, if your child can read, take turns reading.

Pause when you come across a passage or a story that can have more than one interpretation and invites the reader to read between the lines. Look around for clues that might help you draw an inference. For example, in *The New King* by Doreen Rappaport, the story of a king and his son, Prince Rakoto, we are told: "No matter how busy his father was, he always came to take Rakoto to lunch." From this a young reader can infer that because the king took time off to see Rakoto in the middle of his busy schedule, he loved his son very much.

Reread the part of the story you wish to focus on.

Ask questions that prompt your child to think about what is not directly stated on the page. Most versions of *The Princess and the Pea*, for example, don't explain why only a *real* princess can detect a pea underneath twenty fluffy mattresses. What can we infer from this ability? That genuine princesses are more sensitive than other people? That if your blood is truly blue, you will be exceptionally delicate?

Praise answers that are based on information the story provides. If an answer reflects your child's own experience and knowledge, so much the better!

Ask your child to tell *what else* he thinks the writer is really trying to say. In the *Little Engine that Could*, a young reader should understand that the writer is saying everybody should tackle a task with as much determination as the little locomotive.

Don't rush to tell your child what *you* infer. Let him draw his own inferences. Just make sure that whatever the reader says fits in with the story's clues. If your child comes up with something unsupported by the material, ask him to explain how he came to his conclusion.

Readers who can read between the lines learn to:

♦ Spot meaningful clues
♦ Use what they already know to interpret a book
♦ Find more than one meaning in what they read
♦ Identify the main ideas the writer is trying to convey

Example #1

Even old Mother Goose prompts children to read between the lines. Think about this next time you read "Humpty Dumpty" in a typical illustrated edition.

Humpty Dumpty sat on a wall
Humpty Dumpty had a great fall,
All the king's horses and all the
*   king's men,*
Couldn't put Humpty Dumpty
*   together again.*

Focus attention on the picture of Humpty Dumpty.
Ask: What (or who) is Humpty Dumpty? (He's an egg.)
Read between the lines: Why couldn't the king's horses and the king's men put Humpty Dumpty together again? (When an egg falls, it smashes into little pieces and

can't be repaired. You can demon-strate the point next time you break an egg!)

Example #2

An enduring favorite of parents and kids alike is *The Runaway Bunny*, by Margaret Wise Brown. It's a little tale that has a big, reassuring message for very young children.

A little bunny announces to his mother that he is going to run away from home. The mother bunny assures her baby bunny that if he runs away, she'll run right after him and bring him back. What if he turns into a fish and swims away? he asks. Mother Bunny replies that she'll turn into a fisherman and catch him with a rod and reel. What if he turns into a rock on the moun-tainside? She'll climb until she finds

him. What if he turns into a flower? She'll become a gardener and pick him. And so on. In the end, the little bunny concludes that there's no point in running away since he truly belongs with his mother.

Read between the lines: When the little bunny says he wants to run away, why does his mother say she'll bring him back home? (Any number of answers are possible: because she loves him; because she wants to keep him safe; because she thinks he's too young to leave home; because she thinks the world is a dangerous place for little bunnies.)

Why does the little bunny decide not to run away? (He realizes that his mother will just bring him back.) What is the mother bunny really telling her little bunny? (No matter what happens, no matter what he does or where he goes, she'll always be there to take care of him.) Do you think this story could be about people and not just bunnies?

Example #3

James Marshall's wacky adventure *Wings: A Tale of Two Chickens* introduces Harriet, a hen who devotes herself to reading and interesting hobbies, and Winnie, her sister, who prefers to swat flies rather than read and is always bored. The two sisters are as different as two chickens can be.

Pause after the author describes the different natures of the two chickens.

Ask: How are the chickens different? (One does interesting things; the other doesn't do much. One reads; the other doesn't. One gets bored; one never gets bored because she's learning all the time.)

Read between the lines: Which chicken do you think is smarter? (Not Winnie.) Why? (She never does anything interesting; all she does is swat flies.) Which chicken would you rather be? Why?

Read on.

When a stranger, Mr. Johnson, offers Winnie a ride in his helium balloon, she hops cheerfully on board. (The picture shows us that Mr. Johnson is a fox, but Winnie doesn't realize this.)

Focus attention on the picture of the fox.

Ask: What kind of animal is Mr. Johnson?

Read between the lines: Why do you think he wants to take Winnie for a ride? (Foxes love to eat chickens.) Do you think Winnie knows he's a fox? (No.) How can you tell? (She wouldn't have gone with him.) Is Winnie doing something smart or foolish? (Very foolish!) Why do you think so? (He plans to eat her.)

Read on.

Harriet is frantic when she sees her sister flying off with Mr. Johnson. The neighbors aren't surprised. They know Winnie is scatterbrained, but even so she should have known Mr. Johnson was a fox. Harriet explains, "She never reads."

Focus attention on Harriet's answer.

Read between the lines: What does reading have to do with Winnie's bad judgment? (Harriet is really saying that her sister failed to recognize the fox because she probably has never read a book about foxes.)

If Winnie were a reader like her sister, would she have been a smarter chicken? (Certainly. If she were a Real Reader, she would know that chicken is one of a fox's favorite things to eat.)

Ask: What do you think the author is really saying? That it is dangerous for a chicken to go off with a fox? That chickens who read are wiser than chickens who don't? That people who read are wiser than people who don't?

Example #4

In this excerpt from "The Night Before Christmas" (also known as "A Visit from St. Nicholas"), by Clement C. Moore, Real Readers can infer who is telling the story by looking carefully at clues in the poem:

The stockings were hung by the
chimney with care
In the hopes that St. Nicholas soon
would be there.

*The children were nestled all
  snug in their beds,
While visions of sugarplums
  danced in their heads,
And Mama in her kerchief, and I
  in my cap,
Had just settled our brains for a
  long winter's nap. . .*

Ask: Who is the person describing something that happened on Christmas eve?

Read between the lines: Is one of the children telling the story? (No. The storyteller tells us that the children were in bed.) Is Mama telling the story? (No. The storyteller tells us that Mama was in bed in her kerchief.) Then based on the clues, who is probably telling the story? (Probably Poppa—the children's father and Mama's husband, who is snuggled in bed with her, all ready for a "long winter's nap.")

Example #5

One of the very best ways to practice reading between the lines is to ask your child to figure out the moral of a fable or a fairy tale. You might start with Aesop or with Arnold Lobel's contemporary fables, or with a classic tale like Hans Christian Andersen's *The Emperor's New Clothes*.

"Many years ago," Andersen begins, "there lived an emperor who was so fond of new clothes that he spent all his money on finery and costumes." The emperor took no interest in his army, or the theater, or a drive in the park, except when he wanted to show off his new clothes. He had an outfit for every hour of the day. Instead of minding state affairs, he spent almost all of his time in his dressing room.

Along came two clever strangers who, knowing of the emperor's weakness for fancy clothes, claimed they could weave a cloth so magnificent that it could only be seen by the wisest people in the land. But to those who were stupid or not fit for office, the cloth would be invisible. Intrigued, the emperor paid the men a fortune to make a garment from the magical cloth.

In truth, the strangers intended to fool the emperor and all of his court. They set up their looms and ordered the finest silk and golden threads, but they weren't weaving anything. They had a hunch that the emperor's advisors would be afraid to admit they couldn't see fabric on the looms and be thought unfit to serve the emperor. When the strangers presented the "new clothes" to the emperor himself, they knew that he, too, would be ashamed to say he could see nothing. Wouldn't that mean he was stupid and not fit to rule?

In all of the empire, only one person saw through the rascals' trick. When the emperor marched in a parade wearing his "new clothes," a little child pointed out he wasn't wearing anything at all! (After a time, everyone else agreed that the little child was absolutely right.)

Read between the lines: What do you think of the emperor? (Many answers are possible: He's vain; he neglects his duties; he's not a good ruler; he's selfish; he spends money on things that aren't important.)

What did the strangers know? (The strangers knew that they were vain and concerned about what other people would think of them. Rather than risk appearing stupid, everybody would pretend to see something that wasn't there.)

Why is the little child the only one who told the truth? (Andersen seems to think that children are more truthful than adults.)

Do you agree? Why or why not?

Why is it important to learn to say, "I don't think that's true," or "I don't understand"?

What's the moral of this story? (Allow for different interpretations, including: Being vain and selfish will lead you to do foolish things; you shouldn't be afraid of what other people think of you; you should always tell the truth.)

FOLLOW-UP

Drawing inferences from clues is what detectives do to solve crimes. Encourage your child to be a sleuth by making up very simple mysteries for him to solve.

For example, there's a puddle on the rug and a puppy nearby looking a little embarrassed. What can we infer? (The puppy made a mess.)

There's an empty pie tin on the window sill and a squirrel with pie crust in his whiskers. What can we infer? (The squirrel ate the pie.)

It's 9:00 at night and there's a child who's yawning and cranky. What can we infer? (It's time for bed!)

You can use the same read-between-the-lines techniques when you and your child talk about movies, TV shows, songs, or plays. For example, in Walt Disney's animated feature, *Snow White,* the young princess, while fleeing through the forest, comes upon a little cottage in the woods. Nobody is home. After looking around, she concludes that children live there. Why does she make this inference? Is she right?

7 Get the Point

SKILL: IDENTIFYING THE MAIN IDEA

Each of us has been asked and has answered this question more times than we can count. We read something and right away somebody wants to know: *What is it about?*

Explaining what a book or story or article is about is different from restating, or describing what happened. If you were asked to retell the myth of King Midas in your own words, you'd probably say something like this:

Long ago, the Greek god of wine gave King Midas the power to turn everything he touched into gold. At first the greedy Midas was delighted, for he could instantly change twigs, stones, and apples into objects of great value. But soon the king's delight turned to horror. When he sat down to eat, the food and wine hardened into lumps of gold in his mouth; when he hugged his beloved grandchild, she turned into a lifeless golden statue. In the end, poor King Midas begged the god to take away the curse of the golden touch.

That'll do for a retelling. But if you were asked about the *main idea* of the Midas myth, you would talk about it in a more general way, leaving out all but the most important details. You might simply say:

"Having all the gold in the world doesn't bring happiness, and simple things like nourishing food and love are far more important than riches."

Real Readers are in the habit of looking for the main idea. *What is the most important thing this writer is saying?* they ask themselves.

Writers of non-fiction, especially for younger readers, often explain their main ideas in introductory sentences or paragraphs. A title may tell you everything you need to know. When you pick up a book called *Wonderful Worms*, you are sure it's not going to be about sea lions, and you can reasonably expect to find out why the author thinks worms are terrific.

When reading fiction or poetry, however, you may have to hunt around for clues to the main idea. As you read, you need to separate the important details from the minor ones. For example, while it's interesting to know that King Midas first tried out his golden touch on a twig, then on a stone, and then on an apple, these details are *not* the main idea. The main idea is that the power the king thought would make him rich and happy only made him miserable.

It may take a little effort to identify the main idea; but the reward of greater comprehension is worth it. We've often heard about someone who "can't see the forest for the trees." Children can get distracted by all the different kinds of trees, the birds flying overhead, the animals in the underbrush. While these story details are extremely important, children also need to learn that they are all part of the forest! In reading, as in doing jigsaw puzzles, Real Readers know how to make all the pieces add up to one big picture.

Getting the Main Idea

Figuring out the main idea is an active reading skill that is not for beginners except in the very simplest books. Children aren't usually tested in reading comprehension until they are practiced readers. However, you can start working on this skill quite early. When you finish a page or a chapter or a book, just ask this question: *What do you think this is about? What is the main idea?*

See if your child can put the main idea in her own words. If she can't, point in the general direction of the main idea. Here's how:

Skim the book you are about to read together and think about what the main idea may be. Often, the inside book cover will tell you.

Read aloud. If your child can read, take turns reading.

Ask questions that help your child identify signposts to the main point. For example, knowing that King Midas's delight turns to horror when his grandchild becomes a golden statue helps us understand that gold isn't the only thing of value in this world.

Discuss with your child which details are important, which aren't, and why she thinks so.

Prompt your child to express the main idea in her own words.

If your child has trouble understanding how to separate the details from the main point, reread together. Take note of key words here and there and ideas that seem to be connected. Perhaps the title or the first few sentences of the book get straight to the point. Help your child read between the lines, if necessary; perhaps the main idea may be found there.

Readers who can identify the main idea are able to:

- Distinguish between major and minor details
- Draw general conclusions based on specific information
- Think critically
- Remember more of what they read

Example #1

There really *is* a book called *Wonderful Worms*, which is a wonderful introduction to the special role that earthworms play in the natural world. Linda Glaser's simple text and Loretta Krupinski's adorable pictures clearly show young children how plants, animals, and people thrive because the little earthworm is doing its job.

Worms, we discover, have no shovels but they are great diggers, nonetheless. They have no eyes, ears, or noses, but they do have mouths. They use their mouths to eat their way through soil and rotting leaves and dig passageways underground.

They make the soil soft and airy so the roots of plants can breathe and grow. They swallow tiny pieces. And inside the worms, the food changes. When it comes out of their tail end, it makes the earth rich so plants can grow.

Ask: What's this book about? (Earthworms.) Is this fiction or non-fiction? (Non-fiction.) What do you think is the most important thing about earthworms? Not that they don't have eyes, ears, or noses. Not that they don't use shovels. Not that they eat rotting leaves. All these things are good to know. But the main thing about earthworms is that *they make the earth rich so that plants can grow.*

In the back of the book, the author asks and answers some common questions about earthworms, as in the question below. You can practice finding the main idea here, too.

Are there other types of worms? (Yes. There are many types, including roundworms, ribbonworms, flatworms, fanworms, and segmented worms. The earthworm is a type of segmented worm. There are about 12,000 types of segmented worms. A common one is the brandling, which is used for compost. An unusual one that lives in Australia is the giant Australian earthworm. It can grow to be over nine feet long!)

Discuss vocabulary. Work on *segmented*, which means "divided up into little parts" (if you have an earthworm handy, a bicycle chain, or a Tootsie Roll, you can look for the segments). Look up *compost*, a mix of decaying leaves and other organic stuff that can be used as fertilizer.

Focus on the question: Are there other types of worms?

Ask: What should the focus of the answer be? Not the names of the different worms. Not the fact that an Australian worm is nine feet long—even though your child will undoubtedly remember this! Not the fact that the earthworm is segmented. The main idea here is that *there are lots and lots of different kinds of worms.*

Example #2

A clue to the main idea of Esphyr Slobodkina's charming book is in the title: *Caps for Sale: A Tale of a*

Peddler, Some Monkeys and Their Monkey Business. This refashioned version of an old folktale tells of a man who peddles all kinds of caps. He carries them from village to village, very carefully, stacked on his head.

One day, having had no customers all morning, the weary peddler lies down under a tree for a nap. When he awakens, all the caps but his own have mysteriously vanished. It doesn't take long to find the thieves—a gang of monkeys perched high above him in the tree. But try as he may, the peddler can't get the monkeys to return his caps.

When he shouts and shakes his finger at them, they shake their fingers back; when he yells and throws up his hands, so do the monkeys; when he stamps his feet in frustration, they stamp theirs. At last, in anger, the peddler tears off his cap and throws it to the ground. Before he can stomp off, the monkeys throw *their* caps to the ground. Thus, the peddler recovers his caps—through a funny kind of monkey business!

Read the title of the book.

Ask: Do you know what "monkey business" is? (If she doesn't, tell her the story will make it clear.)

Read. If your child can read, take turns reading.

Ask: What is this book about? Not about caps of different sizes and colors, although they're important to the story. Not about the peddler, although the story couldn't happen without him. Not about taking naps under trees.

You have to read between the lines to find the most important idea: *Monkeys mimic what people do.* When the peddler throws down his cap in disgust, the monkeys do the same. Thanks to monkey business, he is able to get his caps back!

Example #3

A lot of kids (not to mention grown-ups) think a cowboy's day is spent chasing stagecoach robbers across the plains or taking on gunslingers in a saloon. In *Cowboys*, written and illustrated by former cowboy Glen Rounds, we get the real story.

Nighttime finds most cowboys in the bunkhouse, reading or playing cards. They get up early in the morning, when it's still dark, and saddle their horses. By the time the sun has risen, the cowboys are already out on the range, eyes peeled for animals that have wandered away. If they spot a stray, they throw a rope around its neck and return it to the herd. After a stampede, they round up the scattered cattle and drive them back to the ranch. Back in the bunkhouse at night, the cowboys relax and wait for supper.

Ask: What is this story about? (A day in the life of a cowboy.) What's the most important thing cowboys do? Not that they read and play cards. Not that they get up real early. Not that they wear big hats. The main idea is: *The cowboys' job is to keep the herd together and catch cows and steers that wander away.*

Example #4

Poetry should be a big part of every child's world of reading. There are many collections of poems in print that will enchant your young reader, from Robert Louis Stevenson's classic *A Child's Garden of Verses* to the whimsical contemporary rhymes of Shel Silverstein's *Falling Up*. There are many fine anthologies, such as *A Child's Treasury of Poems*, with exquisite illustrations from the work of nineteenth-century English artists, and *The Random House Book of Poetry for Children*, edited by Jack Prelutsky, a popular children's poet in his own right, with drawings by the great Arnold Lobel.

A poem is meant to be savored primarily for its sounds and rhythms, the pictures it paints in your mind, and the feelings it evokes. You can deepen your child's appreciation of a beloved poem if you pause to think about what the poet is really saying.

Try this verse, from *A Child's Treasury of Poems*, on your young reader.

The Swallow

—*Christina Rossetti*

Fly away, fly away, over the sea,
Sun-loving swallow, for summer
* is done.*
Come again, come again, come
* back to me,*
Bringing the summer and
* bringing the sun.*

Read the poem once or twice without comment, enjoying its sounds and rhythms.

Ask your child what she thinks the poem is about.

Guide her to understand that the poem is *not* about swallows in particular.

Ask: What is the poet asking the swallow to do first? (Fly away.) What time of year should the swallow fly away? (When summer is done, in the fall when the weather turns cold.)

When should the swallow come back? (Next summer.) When the swallow flies away, what does it mean? (Winter will soon be here.) When the swallow comes back, what does it mean? (Summer is not far away.)

Praise the child who understands that the main idea of the poem is *the end of summer and the changing of the seasons.*

OR

If your child isn't sure about the meaning,

Reread. Before you do, focus her attention on the main idea by asking her to listen for key words that talk about the changing seasons: "Fly away . . . *for summer is done,*" "Come again . . . *bringing the sun.*"

Like "The Swallow," the next poem isn't primarily about the bird in the title.

The Owl

—Anonymous

There was an old owl who lived in an oak;
The more he heard, the less he spoke.
The less he spoke, the more he heard.
Why aren't we like that wise old bird?

Ask: What do you think this poem is about?

Guide the reader to understand the main idea: *In order to learn, it's best to listen more and talk less.* In this poem, the closing question provides the clue to the main idea.

Example #5

Letizia Galli's stunningly illustrated *Mona Lisa: The Secret of the Smile* introduces future art-lovers to Leonardo da Vinci, creator of one of the Western world's most famous paintings.

Da Vinci, who was born in a small Italian town more than five hundred years ago, was always different from everybody else. In school, he amazed his teachers by writing everything backwards! He also embarrassed them by asking lots of questions they could not answer. *Why do birds fly? Why can't plants walk?* the curious boy demanded to know. Leonardo vowed that one day he would find the answers to all these mysteries.

The older da Vinci grew, the odder people thought he was. He wore strange, colorful clothes, he refused to eat anything but vegetables, and he bought birds in the marketplace only to set them free. (He was trying to figure out how they managed to fly.)

His great talent for painting and sculpture also set him apart. Da Vinci was soon in demand to paint portraits of the rich and famous. He also designed fabulous costumes, fireworks, and special displays for the parties and festivals of his wealthy clients.

Da Vinci worked tirelessly to find answers to the riddles of life that intrigued him. He did many experiments and designed things that looked like bicycles, or helicopters, or parachutes—inventions that wouldn't be perfected and used until centuries later. He even made a flying machine based on his observations of birds in flight. The machine didn't work, but it was a good try.

Over his lifetime, da Vinci created beautiful artworks for the churches and palaces of Italy. One of the most famous is the painting of Mona Lisa, a lovely young woman with a mysterious smile that has enchanted viewers for hundreds of years. Today this masterpiece can be seen in the Louvre, the great art museum in Paris, France.

In this book, there is more than one idea worth remembering. By asking different kinds of questions, you can help point your young reader towards different responses.

Ask: What's the most important thing we want to remember about Leonardo da Vinci? Not that he wrote backwards. Not that he was a vegetarian. Not that he wore colorful clothes or watched birds fly.

The title gives us a clue. We want to remember that *da Vinci was a great artist who painted a very famous picture known as the* Mona Lisa.

OR

Ask: According to this book, what is the most important way that da Vinci was different from everybody else? (The book stresses that da Vinci was always *curious* about the world and he was determined to figure out *how things worked*.)

OR

Ask: What were some of the most important things da Vinci did? (He made *great art, like the* Mona Lisa, and he made *a flying machine centuries before airplanes were invented.*)

FOLLOW-UP

Main ideas are not found only in books. They're also to be found in movies and songs and even represented by things such as monuments like the Lincoln Memorial in Washington, DC. Encourage your child to think about hunting for the main idea in many places.

Watching *The Lion King?* Ask the child to tell you *what it is about*, not what happens. (One possible answer: When you're a leader, you have to accept responsibility, be strong, and make wise decisions.)

Singing "You Are My Sunshine"? What is the main idea of the song? (One possible answer: When you love somebody, you don't want them to go away.)

Visiting the Statue of Liberty? What idea does the statue stand for? (One possible answer: The statue shows that the United States welcomes people from other countries to a land of freedom.)

8 Spark the Imagination

SKILL: THINKING CREATIVELY

There are probably millions of perfectly sane little boys and girls who believe that elves frolic under their beds at night or that magical creatures nestle in the closet. There are probably millions more who can conjure up special playmates, fantastic kingdoms, or fabulous adventures. And yet there are many children who need a little help from grown-ups to let imagination take flight.

You may think it's odd for an adult to teach a child how to make believe. You may even suspect that you've gotten a little rusty in the fantasy department. But the secret garden of imagination can be cultivated. Most of us—young, old or in-between—need to keep our imaginations fertile.

Real Readers are constantly using their imaginations: to envision a character or a place described in a book, to fantasize about what they would do if they were a particular character, to imagine a happy ending to a sad story. If a book is particularly wonderful, Real Readers keep it alive in their imaginations long after "The End." Exercising the imagination pays off in a really big way whenever Real Readers sit down to write, whether it's for their own pleasure or in response to an assignment.

You don't have to be a creative genius to spark a child's imagination. With very young children, all that's required is that you be open to a story's possibilities and be willing to spend a little time daydreaming.

As always, start with a few simple, playful ideas. After you have read through a favorite story a few times, prompt your young reader to make a fanciful change or two in the plot. You might ask your child to suggest new places for the main character to visit, new foods for him to eat, or a whole different way of ending the story. *What if . . .* is a good way to begin: *What if* the three bears are at home when Goldilocks arrives at the door of their little cottage? *What if* Little Miss Muffet looks that spider in the eye and doesn't run away?

Simple exercises in fantasy can lead, later on, to inventing a full-blown sequel featuring some or all of the characters in a book. It would be nice, wouldn't it, if the three bears invited Goldilocks in for breakfast? What might happen next? Or what if Sleeping Beauty, upon being kissed awake by the Prince, decides she has no desire to rush into marriage with the first man who asks her. Perhaps she prefers to take a trip around the world before settling down. Can you imagine where she would go? Since the world is now a century older than it was when she fell asleep, how might it be different?

All you have to do is be patient and open to your child's ideas. Give him plenty of time to respond and a few gentle hints if he gets stuck. Sarcasm or ridicule are no-no's; however, you can and should guide your child on his flights of fancy in one important way. While encouraging him to let his imagination roam, prompt him to stay true to the logic of the story or characters. For example, Sleeping Beauty is an ordinary princess, and an ordinary princess can't fly unless a good fairy sprinkles her with fairy dust or she finds a dusty old magic carpet in the attic.

Warning: Once you start imagining, it can be hard to stop!

Sparking Imagination

Even though most children are naturally creative, don't expect your child to be able to talk about his imaginings right off the bat. Some children are shy. Some are afraid they will be laughed at. If at first your child comes up with only a few ideas, or even just a glimmer of an idea, that's just fine. Your job is to provide the right amount of help, the spark that will ignite your child's imagination and help him learn to express himself.

Read aloud. If your child can read, take turns reading.

Start with a favorite book and a favorite character: say, Horton the Elephant in *Horton Hatches the Egg* by Dr. Seuss (see Chapter 2).

Add a new idea to the story each time you reread, and ask your child to do the same. For example, take turns imagining what other problems Horton might face as he's keeping Mayzie's egg warm: a tornado, perhaps, or an avalanche, or an invasion of Martians!

Ask your child to imagine something simple, perhaps that the character is coming over for lunch. What could you make that would please Horton? Peanut butter sandwiches? What if Peter Rabbit were your guest? What kinds of special dishes could you make with carrots?

OR

Change the ending. Perhaps you'll imagine that Hans Christian Andersen's poor little match girl is saved from freezing to death by a rich and lonely old lady; or that Hansel and Gretel don't push the witch into the oven, but use some other trick to get rid of her.

When your child is ready,

Imagine a whole new adventure for a character, from beginning to end. Start off with a problem and guide your child to invent a solution, drawing upon his knowledge and experience.

Say: What if we took Peter Rabbit to the supermarket and he tried to eat all the lettuce. What would the supermarket people do? (Run after him.) What could we do to save him? (Scoop him into our shopping cart and hide him underneath a loaf of bread.) How are we going to get him out of the store? (At the checkout counter we could sneak him into a paper bag.) Are we going to pay for the lettuce he ate?

If your child has trouble coming up with ideas,

Add a detail or two to any little suggestions he makes. For example,

Suggest: Tonight, let's take Peter Rabbit to the circus!

Ask: What would Peter like to see first? If your child says "Lions!" follow his lead.

Add: When Peter gets to the lion's cage, the lion roars and Peter is frightened.

Ask: What does Peter do now? If your child says, "Peter hides,"

Ask: Where? (And so on! Keep adding details and watch the story grow.)

Always look for stories and poems that give children lots of room to imagine. Applaud your child's ideas.

Keep in mind: Too much guidance can squelch your child's imagination; too little may fail to ignite it.

Readers who exercise their imaginations learn to:

- Strengthen verbal skills
- Become good writers
- Solve problems creatively
- Appreciate literature

Example #1

The stupendously stupid Stupid family, whose adventures are presented in a series of hilarious books by Harry Allard, can easily lead to silly imaginings.

In *The Stupids Step Out*, Mr. and Mrs. Stupid, their children, Buster and Petunia Stupid, and their little dog, Kitty, do the dumbest things imaginable. Mrs. Stupid puts on a cat instead of a hat. Mr. Stupid wears stockings on his ears. The whole family takes a bath with their clothes on but they don't fill the tub with water for fear of getting their clothes wet. At the ice cream parlor, they order mashed potato sundaes with butterscotch syrup. And at night, they all sleep together in one bed—backwards—with their feet on the pillow and their heads under the covers.

Imagine you're a member of the Stupid family. What are some silly things that you might do? (Your child shouldn't have much trouble coming up with ideas, but if necessary you can make a few suggestions: Eat dinner while standing on your head, take the goldfish out for a walk, dust the parakeet. The sillier the better!)

Example #2

The Secret in the Matchbox, by Val Willis, boasts a title designed to

97

stimulate your imagination. What can possibly be inside the tiny matchbox that Bobby Bell takes with him to school? Whatever it is, the very sight of it makes Bobby's classmates scream:

The teacher, Miss Potts, takes the matchbox and plunks it on her desk. She doesn't see the tiny dragon creep out. To the children's horror, the busy teacher doesn't notice that the dragon is growing! First, he's no bigger than a shoe; then he's the size of a cat; then he's as big as a dog. And he's breathing fire and smoke!

When Miss Potts finally realizes there's a full-sized fire-breathing dragon in her classroom, she's as terrified as the children. "Do something!" she commands Bobby. At a touch of Bobby's finger, the dragon shrinks until he's tiny enough to pop back inside the matchbox

where, presumably, he remains to this day.

Imagine that you have a magic monster in a matchbox. What kind of monster is it? What color is it? Is it be smooth like a seal? Scaly like a lizard? Can you draw a picture of this monster? What does it eat? How did you find it? How did you trick it into getting into the box? What if it gets out? How will you get your monster back into the box?

Example #3

The haunting children's stories by award-winning writer and illustrator Chris Van Allsburg are always intriguing.

The Wreck of the Zephyr takes us to a fishing village where the remains of a sailboat lie stranded on a high cliff. We wonder how the little boat came to rest there, so far from the sea. An old sailor who is sitting nearby explains.

Years ago, the old man says, a fearless young boy from the village would take his boat out to sea no matter how stormy the weather. Fierce winds and driving rain didn't frighten him at all. "I'm the greatest sailor there is," he would brag.

One day, a terrible storm blew his sailboat, the *Zephyr*, off course. To the boy's surprise, he landed on a mysterious island where sailors far greater than he had learned to fly their boats up into the sky. The boy begged one of the islanders to show him how to sail above the clouds. That night, he slipped aboard the *Zephyr* and magically guided her up toward the stars, toward home. But just as he flew over the rooftops of his village, the wind changed and the boat crashed into the cliff. The boy broke his leg in the fall, the old man concludes, but nobody believed him when he told his story.

The old sailor finishes his tale. He picks up his cane and limps back to the harbor. The wind is rising, and he wants to go sailing.

Imagine you're a sailor who can fly above the clouds. Describe what it feels like to fly in a boat. Is it like riding on a merry-go-round? A ferris wheel? Are there birds passing by? What do they look like? Are you above or below the clouds? What do you see beneath you as you fly? Do you see mermaids and mermen in the waves below? Are they singing to you? If they are, what are they singing? Describe an island you might land on. Are there animals on the island? If there are, what kind? Does anyone live on the island? If there are inhabitants, can you make them your friends? Describe your trip back home.

For a bonus, read between the lines: Who is the old man who is telling the story? (Clues: He's a sailor, like the boy he describes, and he walks with a limp.)

Example #4

If your child would enjoy a poem that's a little on the spooky side, Walter de la Mare's "The Old House," from an illustrated collection of his poems entitled *Peacock Pie*, suggests that strange things are happening behind the front door.

A very, very old house I know—
And ever so many people go,
Past the small lodge, forlorn and
*   still,*
Under the heavy branches, till

Comes the blank wall, and
*   there's the door.*
Go in they do; come out no more.
No voice says aught; no spark of
*   light*
Across that threshold cheers the
*   sight;*
Only the evening star on high
Less lonely makes a lonely sky,
As, one by one, the people go
Into that very old house I know.

Work on new vocabulary, such as *lodge* (a cottage), *forlorn* (sad, deserted), and no voice says *aught* (nobody says anything).

Imagine: You're going into the old house. How old do you think it is? What does it look like? Is it a castle? A cabin? Is it made of glass? Of leaves and grass? Of gingerbread? Who built the house? An ogre? A wicked queen? A lonely prince?

Make up a story about why the _____ (fill in the blank) built the house and why it's now so mysterious. Does the owner live there still? What does the front door look like? What do we see if we peek inside? Does the door take us into a far-away land? If it does, what does it look like? Where do all the people in the poem go? Why don't they ever come out? (They are happy in the wonderful kingdom on the other side of the door; an ogre eats them one by one; they don't remember the magic words that let them out, and so forth.)

Once we've gone through the door, how are we going to get out? (We'll slay the ogre; we'll remember the magic words that open the door; we'll get the help of a fairy godmother . . .)

FOLLOW-UP

Keep a notebook handy to jot down your child's best creative ideas. You may

101

want to compile them in a little book, complete with home-made illustrations. Or you can use pictures cut out of a magazine. (See Chapter 9, "Be a Writer," for more ideas about how to turn a child's imaginings into writing.)

9 Be a Writer

SKILL: CREATING YOUR OWN STORIES

One surefire way to become a Real Reader is to become a Real Writer. Reading and writing go hand in hand because one activity reinforces and enriches the other. Helping your young reader be a young writer isn't as hard as you might think, even if you don't like to write yourself.

Of course, you won't expect your child to be writing bestsellers. You won't even be concerned with spelling, grammar, or any of that other technical stuff. In fact, you won't expect your very young reader to do any writing at all.

You'll be the scribe—jotting down what your child dictates and reading it back to her to make sure you got it right. Eventually you can let her take over the pencil, crayon, pen, or keyboard. But she may not be ready to do this for some time.

For starters, all you need to do is give your young reader the opportunity to think of herself as a writer. You want her to understand that writing is as natural as talking. You also want her to understand that her thoughts, fantasies, and everyday experiences are the

building blocks of books, stories, and poems.

Most important, you are going to read what she has written just as you read anything else! Keep her writings on the shelf next to *Peter Rabbit, Mother Goose, Wonderful Worms*, and other books by famous and not-so-famous authors, and reread her writing from time to time, too.

Having a child create her own material and then hearing it read back is enormously gratifying for both reader and listener. It underscores the idea that reading is a pleasure, not a chore. Having children write stories that reflect what they do, whom they know, and what they know is a foolproof way to engage and hold their interest. It is also a way for children to learn how to share information, feelings, and beliefs.

Just to give you an idea of the kinds of things small children can create, here are some poems and stories dictated by children.

I have a dog whose name is Pete
Who always gets up on my seat.

Dopey, mopey, silly Willy Billy
Ate an ice cream cone,
Dopey, mopey, silly Willy Billy
Now he's done.

Way up in the sky,
I wish I could fly,
But I am a boy
Playing with my toys.

Happy birthday to me,
Happy birthday to me,
I'm having a party,
Come and you'll see.

Elisabeth, the little girl who wrote the following story, even provided a dictionary in which she explained that the blanket was a tissue.

My Life as a Tear

How do you do? I'll ask you first because you are sure not to ask me. There are so many of us. I am the youngest, but there is another coming soon. For you see, I am a tear.

I must tell you a little about myself. I have 34 sisters, 30 brothers, 16 aunts, and 14 uncles.

I have a very short life and quite a lot to see in it.

When I was born, the first thing I saw was a huge white blanket trying to cover me up. I luckily slid away. The next thing that happened was a huge voice saying, "It's not that bad!" The voice sounded like a giant.

I am a sadness tear. People cry sadness tears when they are unhappy. I will live ten tear years. When that time is up, I am usually wiped up with that blanket I was telling you about.

There is another type of tear also. It is a happiness tear. The happiness tears see beautiful things and they live 60 tear years. Happiness tears see everything with a shiny light.

Oh no! The blanket is coming closer and closer. I am trying to slide away but there is not much of me left. I think it is time to say goodbye!

Children who create their own stories learn to:

♦ Express thoughts and feelings
♦ Stretch their imaginations
♦ Gain a sense of control of language
♦ Become better readers

Becoming a Writer

There are many ways to prompt your child to write. How you go about doing this depends, as does everything else you do with a young person, on the child's age, maturity, and verbal ability.

Sometimes it's fun to follow an activity with writing. You may simply decide to jot down notes, or you may prefer to write a paragraph or two about what you've just done. When you do this regularly, writing becomes "doing what comes naturally."

Start simply.

Expand writing activities gradually.

Write exactly what your child dictates. This is her story, not yours.

If your child is a beginning writer, don't correct spelling or grammar. School will address these later on. Your only job is to make sure you understand what she has written so that you can read it back the way she dictated it.

If you do write or type up your child's writing, you can correct spelling as needed if you really can't resist! However, you must respect your child's style and choice of words, even if these don't, strictly speaking, make sense.

Add a title page, with the young author's name prominently displayed in bright colors, illustrations (home-made photos or drawings, or pictures cut from a magazine), and maybe a table of contents.

If your child can identify different kinds of writing (see Chapter 3),

Ask: What have you written? Fiction? Non-fiction? A poem? A biography? An autobiography?

Just as reading opportunities abound, so do writing opportunities. The following examples suggest some things to try that will surely prompt your young reader to think of herself as a writer, too. You are going to be pleasantly surprised at how easy it is to find opportunities to incorporate writing into your child's day.

Write Every Day

Write to remember: Out of ice cream, cereal, bananas? Let's write a shopping list so we don't forget to buy what we need at the supermarket.

Throughout the year, there'll be plenty of lists to write. Here are some: books to look for at the library, a list of Christmas presents, a Thanksgiving menu shopping list, a list of people to invite to a birthday party, a packing list.

Write to tell: Going to be back late? Let's leave a note for Mom to tell her where we're going. Write a note to the baby-sitter to make sure she knows there's strawberry ice cream in the freezer.

Write to surf: Get e-mail? Let's e-mail someone in cyberspace—maybe someone who lives as far away as Katmandu.

Write up a special occasion or outing. For example, take some photos while visiting the zoo. Have your youngster write about what you saw and write a caption for each picture, according to her ability. Then have her read it all back to you.

Make a birthday book out of her next birthday party. Tell who came, what games were played, what the birthday cake looked like, and what presents she got. Send a copy to an absent grandparent or other relative. Bet you'll get a reply!

Keep a Diary

When your child is old enough to describe what she did during the day, get a loose-leaf binder or one of those nicely bound books with blank pages. Ask if she'd like to keep a diary or start her autobiography. She'll probably jump at the chance.

Once a week or so, prompt your child to tell you the most exciting, sad, funny, or interesting thing that happened recently. It might be something that struck her fancy during the day, like a game she enjoyed at the playground or a visit with a friend.

On a fresh page of the diary, write the date and write down what your child has to say. It's important to record *her exact words*, even if they're a little hesitant or roundabout. At first, a sentence or two is fine. As your child gets older, gently prompt her to add details and clarify.

Remember to Resist the urge to correct grammar. Don't impose your ideas or vocabulary. It's okay if she says, "I seen a tiger at the zoo." The words must belong entirely to your child.

Read the entry back just as it was dictated.

Ask: Is there anything you want to change or add?

Leave room for photographs, illustrations, and captions. Scribbles are just fine.

Reread from time to time. For example, on the first of each month, you can review the past month's worth of days, reminding your child that this is her very own diary.

Double the fun: Keep a double diary. You write an entry for every one written by your child. Keep yours simple and mostly about her! Describe events using colors, sounds, and smells.

Your child will pick up a lot about writing from seeing you do it. For example: Your child might dictate, "Me saw turtle." Your entry might be: "Thursday afternoon we went to the pet store. We saw a big green turtle sitting on a rock and Kim asked what turtles like to eat."

For somewhat older readers, start a **Q & A journal**. Take turns writing Questions and Answers. For example, you write, "What is your favorite game?" and your child writes a response. Then she makes up a question for you, and you reply in writing.

Write Book Reports

This is where restating skills (see Chapter 4) and identifying the main idea (see Chapter 7) pay off.

When you've finished a story or book or poem,

Ask your child to retell it in her own words (which you'll faithfully record).

Prompt your child to be a critic (see Chapter 10). Award one, two, or three stars (you can get stickers or a rubber stamp) to the books you have reviewed.

Write a Story

When your child is ready, prompt her to invent a story from beginning to end. She can start by spinning a new tale about a favorite character from a book or movie.

One good way to get started is to take a simple story as a model.

Example #1

In *A Snowy Day*, author Ezra Jack Keats tells of a boy named Peter who awakens one wintry morning to find that snow has fallen during the night.

The writer follows Peter throughout his day. Peter puts on his snowsuit and goes outside to play. He makes tracks in the snow and knocks snow the branches of a tree with a stick. He makes a snowman and sees older boys having a snowball fight.

When Peter gets home, his mother plops him right into a warm bathtub. Once tucked into bed, he worries that all the lovely snow will be gone in the morning. But when he wakes up there is still snow everywhere, and new flakes are falling.

Say: This is a story about a snowy day. What kind of day would you like to write about? A sunny day? A rainy day? A beach day? How about a silly day? A boring day? A dopey day? The day you learned to ride your bike? A day at Grandma's house?

Start with getting up in the morning and end with going to bed at night.

Prompt your child to include *who* is in the story and *where* and *when* the story is taking place. Remember to think about who is telling the story (see Chapter 5).

Example #2

Here's another book you can take as a model. In *Frog and Toad Together*, Arnold Lobel tells four little stories about these two amphibian friends. In "A List," Toad realizes that he has a great many things to do. He decides to write them down on a list in order to make sure he remembers them.

After he has done each one, he crosses out the activity. For example, after he gets up and eats breakfast, he crosses out "Eat breakfast."

Frog and Toad are taking a walk together ("Take walk with Frog") when a gust of wind blows Toad's list of things to do right out of his hand. Frog shouts that they should go and get it, but Toad says no, he can't, because running after his list isn't on his list of things to do. Without his list, Toad feels that he has no choice but to sit and do nothing, so that's what he does. Frog sits and does nothing with him.

When it starts to get dark, Frog tells Toad that it is time to go to sleep. This reminds Toad that "Go to sleep" was the last item on his list. He writes "Go to sleep" on the ground with a stick. Then he crosses it out and the two friends lean up against a tree and go to sleep.

Ask: Do you think Toad was sensible or silly when he could not do anything without his list? Do you have a number of things to do today? Would a list be a helpful thing to have?

Say: Let's make a list of things to do and cross out each one as we do it.

The list might look like this:

SATURDAY
Get up.
Get dressed.
Have breakfast.
Brush teeth.
Go to the supermarket.
Go to the drugstore.
Buy a present for Robbie.
Play on the swings.
Visit Uncle Andrew.
Have lunch.
(and so on, until bedtime)

Imagine other list-makers, such as a baby elephant and a crocodile. A baby elephant might put "Eat peanuts" on his list. A crocodile might put "Eat baby elephant" on his!

Write a list of things to do for someone (like a pet, Grandma or Grandpa, or a baby-sitter).

If you play a "Pretend" game, you will never run of out things to write.

Pretend you are a freckle, an eyelash, or a toe. Your young reader chooses the body part that's going to tell the story. Knowing about point-of-view comes in handy here (see Chapter 5). Reread *My Life as a Tear* at the beginning of this chapter to see how one parent wrote up her child's imaginings.

Pretend you have found a strange animal and are writing a story about it for someone who has never seen it. Maybe it's a reptile with the head of an ostrich and the feet of a tiger.

Ask: What is this strange animal called? (A tigrich? An ostrile?) What does it look like? What does it eat?

Pretend you live somewhere else, real or imaginary.

Ask: What kind of place is it? What does it look, feel, and smell like? What do you all day? Who else lives there?

Be a Poet

*Children quickly learn to see
That poems are easy as can be,
And when a little rhyme is done,
You've had an awful lot of fun.
Yes, every child can be a poet
If someone only lets them know it!*

Long before toddlers stop toddling and approach school age, poetry comes naturally. Children love to rhyme; "Roses are red/Violets are blue/Sugar is sweet/There's goo on your shoe" is the way one youngster finished the familiar verse. If you read a poem with a strong rhyming sequence and catchy rhythm, you will find that children remember it readily and can fill in the end words by the second or third hearing. All they need is opportunity and encouragement.

As your taking-off point, use good old *Mother Goose* or any of the many other poems written for young children. One of the nicest collections of contemporary children's poetry is *Father Fox's Pennyrhymes* by Clyde Watson. Almost every opening line is an invitation for a young reader to think like a poet. Here are a few beginnings from *Father Fox*, with children's lines in parentheses.

> *The sky is dark, there blows a*
> *storm,*
> *(I'm glad my house is nice and*
> *warm.)*

> *The rain falls down*
> *The wind blows up,*
> *(I have chocolate ice cream in a*
> *cup.)*

> *Knock! Knock! Anybody there?*
> *(Look! It's a big brown bear!)*

> *Huckleberry, gooseberry,*
> *raspberry pie,*
> *(Appleberry, chocolateberry,*
> *blueberry pie.)*

> *Ding, Dong,*
> *Sing me a song,*
> *(I love you, you love me, we're a*
> *happy family.)*

> *There were five fellows*
> *Went to a fair,*
> *(One, two, three, four, five.)*

Try these openers out on your child and compile her responses in a little book. From here it's just one baby step to composing original poems!

Write Letters

The Jolly Postman by Janet and Allan Ahlberg is a book about the many different kinds of letters the postman delivers in a day. In this book, which

older children will enjoy, readers get to look into envelopes and pull out each piece of mail. The details reward a close look: For example, the postmark on the letter from Jack (of beanstalk fame) reads "East of Sun, West of Moon."

The three bears get a letter from Goldilocks saying she's sorry for breaking into their house and eating baby bear's porridge. At the gingerbread cottage, home of the wicked witch, the postman delivers an advertising flier from Hobgoblin Supplies Ltd. Jack has sent a postcard to the giant: Thanks to the hen that lays golden eggs, Jack and his mother are off on a grand tour.

At the palace of Her Royal Highness, Cinderella, the postman delivers a little fairy tale that is awfully biographical. The big bad wolf gets a lawyers' notice to stop bothering Little Red Riding Hood's grandmother and also letting him know that the three little pigs are planning to sue. The last thing the postman brings is a birthday card to Goldilocks, who is seven, which is just about the right age for this little book.

Go through the mail and talk about all the different kinds of letters that come to your house (for example, bills, advertisements, notices, correspondence, magazines, postcards, invitations, thank you notes, greeting cards).

Prompt your child to write a response to a letter, card, or an invitation.

Miss a friend who moved away? Send a postcard or letter. Write to a character in a favorite book or story or on TV; to a cherished pet, real or stuffed; to the President of the United States.

Ask a friend or relative to be your child's penpal and encourage him or her to correspond regularly.

10 Think It Over

SKILL: BEING A CRITIC

Real Readers love to read because they are good at it. When they pick up a book, they know they have effective strategies to use on any reading challenge they encounter. The more they read, the more they develop a context, "a reading neighborhood," in which to put the books they've read. This means that the reader who has read a lot of dinosaur books approaches a new dinosaur story with confidence.

However, Real Readers don't necessarily like or believe everything they read. They are not simply receptacles for ideas that have found their way into print. On the contrary, Real Readers *think critically* about every book, *comparing* and *contrasting* it with similar books they have read and deciding whether it is interesting or boring, believable or unbelievable.

Right from the outset, your child should be encouraged to be a critical reader. When you've reached "The End," always ask: *What do you think about this book?* As soon as your young reader has a few books under his belt, especially if these books have similarities, you can ask: *Which book did you like better? Why?*

If you think your young reader isn't old enough to make critical judgments and express his opinions, think again. Children are extremely opinionated. They pick and choose all the time: the foods they'll eat, the toys they'll play with, the people they like. Once you start reading with children, you will discover that, with a little prompting and direction, they are quite happy to be opinionated about books as well.

Even if you haven't asked directly, you are probably already aware of your child's literary tastes. Young readers have favorite books that they want to hear over and over and over again. If you ask, your child may be able to explain what he likes so much about a beloved story. If he has trouble explaining, you can help him by asking questions about specific parts of the story—the characters, the plot, the title, the ending. Ask him to tell what he likes and why he likes it.

Just as important, you can ask your child to explain why he does *not* like a book. He might say, "There are not enough pictures," or "It's too boring," or "The end is silly," or "The story is too babyish." Keep his critiques in mind when you select the next book for him to read.

"I like the bed part," says one little girl who is hooked on *Peter Rabbit*. When prompted, she explains that she loves the end when naughty Peter—who disobeyed his mother's warning, sneaked into Mr. McGregor's garden and nearly got caught—has to go to bed early while his brothers and sisters have bread, milk, and blackberries for supper. "It's only fair," the young reader insists. In other words, she likes the ending because it appeals to her sense of justice.

There are big dividends to be gained from guiding young readers to be critics. Your child will be more inclined to read and to enjoy reading if he knows that you honor his likes and dislikes and take his opinions seriously. As children move up the academic ladder, they are going to be bombarded with assignments and tests that require them to make critical judgments about what they have read. Anything you can do to help your child put a foot on the path to critical thinking is a fine idea.

Developing Critical Skills

Don't misunderstand. Criticizing something just for the sake of criticizing is not the point. Nor should you impose *your* opinions, although you certainly have a right to express them, and you should! Your job is to guide your young reader to think along these lines:

I think about what I read after I've read it. What I think is important. I can pick out what I like about a story and what I don't like. If I've read a similar book, I can decide if I like one better and say why. Or, I can decide I like both books for different reasons. When I read something new and different, I can decide whether I would like to read something else on the same subject or by the same author.

Readers who think critically learn to:

♦ Notice details
♦ Compare one thing with another
♦ Generalize
♦ Have confidence in their own judgment

When you are reading a new book,

Talk about what the book is about and who wrote it.

Remember whether you have read any other books by the same writer or books that remind you of the one you are reading now.

Read aloud. If your child can read, take turns reading.

Ask: Is this a good book? What do you like about it? What don't you like? (The title? The characters? The ending?) If there are pictures, do they work well with the story? Is this a book about real people and things (non-fiction) or a book that someone has imagined (fiction)? Which do you prefer? Do you think this book is too short? Do you wish it had gone on longer? Do you like books written by this author?

Let's say that you've just finished a Halloween book, a ghost story filled with creepy creatures.

Ask: What kind of book is this? (Scary, weird.) Who wrote it? Do you like scary books? Why or why not? Do you want to look for other books about witches and goblins? Have you read any other books you thought were scary? If you have, which was scarier?

For more experienced readers: Can you tell me how this book differs from some other scary book that you have read? (It has a different ending; this book is longer; it has pictures; it's in rhyme; it comes with a face-painting kit; in this book, the little girl's name is Annie, but in the other book, there's a little boy named Jake; and so on!)

Praise the reader for the differences noted, whether significant or small. He's exercising his critical faculties in every case.

Note: For quite a long time, if you ask, *Is this a good book?* the answer you get will be "yes." This is partly because this is what your child thinks you want to hear, and partly because your child hasn't read enough to discriminate between one book and another. Don't stop asking! One of these days, he's going to say no and, if asked, will be happy to tell you why.

Compare books by the same author. This is a simple, natural way to bring out the critic in even a very young reader. It's easy to do if all the books have a similar format. For example, author Eve Tharlet has written a series: *I Wish I Were . . . a Bird, . . . A Mouse, . . . A Lion*, and *. . . a Baby*.

In each of these books, a youngster is discontented for some reason and thinks that if only he were something else he would be happier. A bird has the kind of freedom a small child cannot have. A mouse has no responsibilities and can play all day. A lion isn't afraid of anyone and does just as he pleases. A baby gets all the attention. At the close of each book, the child realizes that there are drawbacks to being a bird, a mouse, a lion, or a baby, and big advantages to being a child.

Ask: Which book do you like best? Why? Which book do you like least?

Why? Can you think of anything else a child might wish to be? (A puppy, a flower.) What is the same about these books? What is different?

Compare books with similar themes: Let's say your child has really gotten a kick out of *The Escape of Marvin the Ape* (see Chapter 5) and can't seem to hear it often enough. You can look for another book about apes or other animals who escape from the zoo.

How about *Good Night, Gorilla*, by Peggy Rathmann? On the very first page, a caged gorilla steals the keys out of the zookeeper's pocket even as the zookeeper is saying, "Good night, Gorilla." In the pages which follow, we watch the zookeeper as he walks along saying good night to the elephant, the lion, the hyena, the giraffe, and the armadillo. Trailing behind, freeing each animal, is the gorilla, until we have a little parade led by the unsuspecting zookeeper.

The animals follow him right into his house, right up into the bedroom where his wife is drifting off to sleep. Each animal finds a place to curl up. A little mouse snuggles in a night-table drawer, and the gorilla gets right into bed with Mrs. Zookeeper who, thinking it is her husband, murmurs, "Good night, dear."

Upon hearing a whole chorus of "Good night's," she turns on the light. She gets right up and leads the parade of sleepy animals back to the zoo. "Good night, zoo," she says, unaware that the gorilla is still right behind her. In the very last picture, Mr. and Mrs. Zookeeper are in bed and the gorilla is tucked in between them. So is the mouse, who says, "Good night, Gorilla."

Ask: Do you like *Good Night, Gorilla*? Why or why not? How is *Good Night, Gorilla* different from *The Escape of Marvin the Ape*? (The gorilla steals the zookeeper's keys, Marvin just slips out; the gorilla lets a lot of animals escape, only Helvetica the hippo escapes at the end of the story; the gorilla goes to the zookeeper's house, Marvin goes out on the town.) How are the two books similar? (They are both about very large monkeys; they both start out in the zoo; they both have a zookeeper in them; there are color pictures in both books; both the gorilla and Marvin act more like people than like animals; at the end of each book, both Marvin and the gorilla are still free.)

Praise your child for differences and similarities noticed.

Remember: What is important is the idea of thinking about one book in relation to another.

Ask: Which book did you like better? Why? (One reader preferred *The Escape of Marvin the Ape* because Marvin gets to go to lots of places, while the gorilla just goes to sleep. Another reader liked *Goodnight, Gorilla* because he thought it was hilarious when the gorilla got into bed with Mrs. Zookeeper.)

Compare different versions of the story. If your young reader is advanced, he may be interested in reading several different editions of the same tale. Aesop's *Fables* come in many versions, in poetry and in prose. You could follow up a simple biography of Paul Revere, such as *A Picture Book of Paul Revere* by David Adler, with Henry Wadsworth Longfellow's poem, "Paul's Revere's Ride." Or you could read "The Pied Piper of Hamelin," a children's poem by Robert Browning, after you've read the illustrated prose version by Sara and Stephen Corrin.

If your child enjoyed Rudyard Kipling's *The Elephant's Child* (see Chapter 1), try *How the Ostrich Got Its Long Neck*, a Kenyan folktale retold by Verna Aardema. Just like the elephant's child, whose trunk was stretched to its present length by a hungry crocodile, the ostrich had a short neck until a crocodile beseeched the silly bird to take a look at a sore tooth in the back of its mouth.

After reading both versions,

Discuss which one your young reader liked best, and why. He can like both of them equally, of course.

Compare pictures of the elephant's trunk and the ostrich's neck.

Compare the cast of characters in each book. Which animals does your child like best?

Along the same lines, follow up a reading of the classic fairy tale *Rumplestiltskin* with *Paco and the Witch*, a Puerto Rican folktale retold by Felix Pitre.

In Paul O. Zelinksy's lovely retelling of *Rumplestiltskin*, a poor miller lies to a king that his beautiful daughter can spin straw into gold. The king locks the girl in a room filled with straw and orders her to spin it into gold overnight or be put to death in the morning. Luckily, a little man with magical powers comes to her rescue and spins a roomful of gold for three nights straight.

For his services, the little fellow demands something of value: a necklace or a ring. On the third night, having nothing left to offer, the girl is forced to promise that she will give the little man her first child.

Soon afterwards, the miller's daughter marries the king and bears him a son. Rumplestiltskin appears to claim the child, and tells the queen he will release her from her vow only if she can guess his name. Although she wracks her brain, she cannot guess it. In the nick of time, a faithful servant discovers the little man's secret: Rumplestiltskin is his name!

Paco and the Witch is set on the island of Puerto Rico, where Paco, a little boy, lives with his family. Lurking in the woods near their village is a wicked *bruja*, which is how you say *witch* in Spanish.

One day while running an errand for his mother, Paco comes across the *bruja* disguised as a helpless old woman. She takes him prisoner and tells him he will be hers forever unless he can guess her name. Like the miller's daughter, Paco hasn't a clue.

When the evil hag (who is planning to eat Paco for dinner) sends him to the river for water, the weeping, homesick boy is befriended by a *cangrejo*, or crab, who reveals the *bruja's* name: *Casi Lampu'a Lentemue*.

The spell is broken. Paco goes free while the furious witch chases the crab with a stick. This is why, to this day, crabs always scuttle under rocks when they see people coming!

After reading the two stories,

Prompt your child to talk about the similarities and differences. Where and when does each story take place? Who are the characters in each story? How does the miller's daughter discover the little man's name? How does Paco learn the *bruja's* name?

Compare the characters with mysterious names: the one a little man, the other a witch. Whose name is weirder? Are they both wicked? Which character is scarier? Why?

Compare points of view. Why did the miller lie to the king about his daughter? How did the miller feel when the king threatened to put his daughter to death if she didn't spin straw into gold? How did the miller's daughter feel about her father's big lie? How did Paco's family feel when he disappeared? Why did the crab help Paco?

Prompt imagination by asking your child to make up a mysterious name for himself. Then try to guess it!

Discuss which story your young reader likes better and why.

FOLLOW-UP

Each time you and your youngster finish a new book, see a new movie, listen to a new song, or play a new game, ask: *What do you think about that?*

Encourage him to express his opinions freely. If appropriate, guide him to relate the new book, movie, song, or game to something he has read, seen, heard, or played before.

Feel free to share your opinions without imposing them. The idea is to engage your child in a lively, open-ended discussion.

PART

three:

- The *Really Reading!* Bookshelf
- Books Discussed

The *Really Reading!* Bookshelf

The *Really Reading!* Bookshelf is stocked with books that work particularly well with *Really Reading!* strategies. They also happen to be books that we think your child will find fun to read!

Will these books appeal to *your* reader? Maybe, maybe not. You'll just have to try, and the earlier you start, the better. (For some children, eighteen months is not too early.) As you and your child read together, you will get to be an expert at choosing books your child will love.

The books on the shelf range from fiction to non-fiction, poetry to fairy tales. We indicate which are suitable for beginning readers, which are suitable for more advanced readers, and which are suitable for in-between readers. Keep in mind that suggested reading levels only reflect a general idea of how easy or difficult a book is and whether the subject or story is likely to be of interest. And of course, you have to take into account whether you are doing the reading or the child is reading on his own.

We can all agree that some books, like *Goodnight, Moon,* are for very young readers and others, like *Moby Dick,* are for very grown-up readers. But there are many books (in fact, some of the most resonant and beloved books) that refuse to fall neatly into any one category. The works of E. B. White, for example—*Charlotte's Web*, *Stuart Little*, and *The Trumpet of the Swan*—are enjoyed and revisited by an enormously wide spectrum of readers, from second or third graders to adults.

So follow your nose—and your young reader's. Most of the writers noted have many books to their credit. If your reader really gets a kick out of Gene Zion's *Harry the Dirty Dog*, for instance, this is your cue to see if there are other books in which Harry makes an appearance. (There are.) There are also many non-fiction series, from biology to biography, that you can explore.

Most important, don't get into a reading rut. A big part of your job is to select books that stretch your young reader's capabilities and add to his or her store of knowledge.

A NOTE ABOUT AGE AND SKILL LEVELS

Our bookshelf is broken down into groups based on readiness levels: *Beginner*, *Intermediate*, and *Advanced*. Keep in mind the following when deciding on the appropriate level for your child:

Beginners are just getting the hang of what books are about and are learning basic reading readiness skills. They are not reading on their own yet (or at least they are not reading the printed words on the page!) and will need to be read to by an adult or older child. *Beginners'* ages range from two to five years old.

Intermediates can read a bit on their own, but are still mostly read to. They are not entirely at ease with reading yet, and rely on active adult participation. *Intermediates'* ages range from four to seven years old.

Advanced readers still enjoy being read to, but are able readers on their own. While we all know some very young children who can read independently, advanced readers are usually at least five, and are mostly six or seven years old. An eight-year-old child who is not yet an *Advanced* reader should probably be evaluated by a school professional to determine whether special direction or tutoring is needed.

CHAPTER 1: GUESS WHAT HAPPENS NEXT!

Predictable books, which are mostly for beginning readers, are easy to find. As your child matures, you can practice the skill of prediction with almost any book that has a strong story.

For Beginners

The Circus Baby by Maude and Miska Petersham (Aladdin, 1989). Mother Elephant admires the way Mr. and Mrs. Clown feed their baby. What happens when she tries to feed her baby the same way?

Five Minutes' Peace by Jill Murphy (Putnam, 1986). Mrs. Large, an aptly named elephant mother, tries in vain to find some quiet, private time in her own house. Will she succeed?

Harry the Dirty Dog by Gene Zion (HarperCollins, 1956). Harry, a white dog with black spots and a serious dislike of baths, gets really dirty. What will happen?

Owl Babies by Martin Waddell (Candlewick Press, 1975). Sarah, Percy, and Bill, three little owls, worry when their owl mother is nowhere to be found. Will she return?

The Very Lonely Firefly by Eric Carle (one of the examples in this chapter) is part of a series that includes *The Very Hungry Caterpillar*, *The Very Quiet Cricket*, and *The Very Busy Spider* (Philomel). If your child loved *Firefly*, she'll enjoy the others. All are based on repeatable and predictable patterns.

For Intermediate Readers

The Biggest Bear by Lynd Ward (Houghton Mifflin, 1952). Johnny goes hunting for bear and catches a cub. As the little bear grows, so does his appetite. Soon he's an enormous creature, eating Johnny and his family out of house and home. Johnny is told to take his pet back to the woods. What happens next?

Mike Mulligan and His Steam Shovel by Virginia Lee Burton (Houghton Mifflin, 1939). Mike and his steam shovel, Mary Anne, face one last challenge on their way to a new career. Will they manage to dig the cellar for the Popperville town hall? If they do, how will they get out?

Millions of Cats by Wanda Gag (Sandcastle, 1928). A little old woman yearns for a cat, and her devoted husband sets off to find one. He comes to a place with millions of cats. Which will he choose?

For Advanced Readers

Miss Rumphius by Barbara Cooney (Viking, 1982). Little Alice's grandfather is an artist who paints pictures of ships and the sea. He tells her that when she grows up, she must "do something to make the world more beautiful." Ask what Alice can do—and what your young reader can do—to make the world more beautiful.

Something Is Going to Happen by Charlotte Zolotow (HarperCollins, 1988). The whole family senses that something is in the air. What can it be? You'll have to pay close attention to predict the answer.

CHAPTER 2: WHAT DOES THIS MEAN?

Don't shy away from books with words slightly above your children's level. That's how young readers stretch.

For Beginners

Camel Caravan by Bethany Roberts and Patricia Hubbell (Tambourine, 1996). Here's an opportunity for a young reader to think of all the words that rhyme with *clump*. We follow the clumping camels as they sneak out of the desert and *thump* around the world in search of greener pastures.

The Cat in the Hat Beginner Dictionary by the Cat Himself and P. D. Eastman (Random House, 1964). This is lots of fun: a decidedly unstuffy and somewhat unpredictable dictionary with amusing definitions and illustrations.

My First Dictionary by Betty Root (Dorling Kindersley, 1993). This attractive dictionary has detailed pictures and photographs set against a bright white background.

Red Cat, White Cat by Peter Mandel (Holt, 1994). Opposites make an appearance in easy-to-read-and-remember rhymes with playful illustrations.

For Intermediate Readers

Rotten Island by William Steig (Viking, 1984). An award-winning author of many outstanding books for children, Steig never talks down to his young readers. The words he uses to tell his whimsical stories are as colorful as his pictures.

In this eye-catcher, hateful monsters thrive in a rotten, horrible place full of lava-spewing volcanoes and boiling seas. Steig's illustrations of disgusting monsters will grab your child's attention. So will a wealth of words like *glimmered, denizens, talons, tentacles,* and *sauerkraut.* (As a bonus, ask your child to predict what will happen to the monsters.)

Runnery Granary by Nancy Farmer (Greenwillow, 1996). Something or somebody has been eating the grain in the Runnery's granary (look for the context clues). Other excellent words: *weevils, fetched, smithereens, yowled,* and the word for the ones whodunit.

Zinnia and Dot by Lisa Campbell Ernst (Puffin, 1995). Two vain hens sit on their nests. Each boasts that her eggs are more beautiful. Then a weasel runs off with all but one of the eggs. Whose egg is it? This book has delicious words like *alabaster, shimmer, display,* and *poultry pandemonium.*

For Advanced Readers

Antics, by Cathi Hepworth (Putnam and Grosset, 1992). You've probably never given a thought to all the words that have ants in them. Here is **ant**ique (a grandma ant knitting; brilli**ant** (an Einstein-y ant with a test tube full of discoveries); ench**ant**er (an ant-wizard) and many more.

The Night I Followed the Dog by Nina Laden (Chronicle, 1994). A suburban dog lives a humdrum doggy life by day but lives it up at night. Words are presented in artistic ways that illustrate their meaning.

The Star-Spangled Banner by Frances Scott Key, illustrated by Peter Spier (Doubleday, 1973). Did you ever stop to think about the words in our national anthem? Sing along as you find the meaning of *perilous, ramparts, gallantly, star-spangled!*

Zin! Zin! Zin! A Violin by Lloyd Moss (Simon & Schuster, 1995). This is a sprightly introduction to the names of musical instruments and groups of musicians—from solo to octet to orchestra, and from bassoon to flute to violin. Marjorie Priceman's enthusiastic illustrations are a big plus.

CHAPTER 3: TELL THE DIFFERENCE

When grown-ups pick out books for young readers, they usually reach for fiction. This is partly out of habit and partly because most children's classics are made-up stories.

Break the fiction habit! Broaden your children's reading experiences by bringing home lots of different kinds of books. You will enrich their vocabulary and expand what educators like to call *the knowledge base.* Also, you are likely to hit on some subjects that really engage your young readers.

Next time you go to the bookstore or library, look beyond the fiction shelves. You'll be amazed at the variety of children's books available at all reading levels. There's no reason to think little boys and girls will be any less enchanted by a book about walking on the moon than by a tale of cuddly bunnies!

Non-fiction

Here are some popular topics: history, other countries, science, art and artists, music and musicians, transportation, the way things work, the way things are made, food, sports.

Poetry

Poems for children come in all shapes and sizes. Anything or anyone can be the subject of a poem.

Sing a Song of Popcorn—Every Child's Book of Poems (Scholastic, 1958) is a particularly nice anthology, illustrated by nine Caldecott Medal-winning artists. Another excellent collection is *The Random House Book of Poetry for Children* (Random House, 1983), edited by Jack Prelutsky. There's something for every reading level in these anthologies.

Some other child-tested books of poetry for readers of all ages are *A Child's Garden of Verses* by nineteenth-century author Robert Louis Stevenson (Delacorte, 1985), and *Falling Up* by contemporary author Shel Silverstein (HarperCollins, 1996).

Magazines

There are racks full of periodicals for children, some even for very young ones. A children's librarian can help you find the right magazine for your child and, since kids love to get mail, a subscription makes a great gift.

Biographies/Autobiographies

Stories about real people can be every bit as dramatic as fiction. This is a clever way to get your child hooked on history.

CHAPTER 4: SAY IT IN YOUR OWN WORDS

When looking for books for your child to retell, keep an eye out for stories with a strong sequence of events to help build memory.

For Beginners

The Carrot Seed by Ruth Krauss (HarperCollins, 1945). A little boy plants a carrot seed. Even though all the grown-ups laugh and say it will never sprout, the boy tends it lovingly, and a huge carrot grows.

Dear Zoo by Rod Campbell (Four Winds Press, 1982). What are you going to do when the zoo keeps sending you the wrong pet? This is a lift-the-flap book that can also be used to practice prediction.

Dinosaur Time by Peggy Parrish (Harper & Row, 1974). Small dinosaur lovers will love this non-fiction book, which provides opportunities for restating what the book has to say about a number of different dinosaurs.

Guess How Much I Love You by Sam McBratney (Candlewick Press, 1994). Little Nutbrown Hare and Big Nutbrown Hare are having an unusual contest. They are trying to out-love one another. It's hard to resist acting this out as you restate.

For Intermediate Readers

After the Flood by Arthur Geisert (Houghton Mifflin, 1994). Any child who ever wondered about what happened to Noah and his family after they reached dry land will enjoy this beautifully illustrated Bible tale.

Angelina Ballerina by Katharine Holabird (Clarkson N. Potter, 1983). Angelina is a mouse who yearns to dance. This story about how Angelina becomes a famous ballerina is fun to retell and has many good vocabulary words in it. There are more Angelina adventures.

Bread Is for Eating by David and Phillis Gershator (Holt, 1995). We follow a seed from planting to growing wheat, to milling, to baking, and finally to eating. You can retell the tale of how bread gets to the table—and sing the Spanish song that inspired the story.

Three Billy Goats Gruff by Paul Caldone (Clarion, 1973). Clever goats find a way to get the better of a scary troll who threatens to eat them.

For Advanced Readers

Fables by Arnold Lobel (Harper Collins, 1980). All of these witty original fables are fun to read and fun to retell. Hold on to this book for when you practice looking for the main idea (Chapter 7).

Stone Soup by Marcia Brown (Scribners, 1947). Three hungry soldiers find a clever way to outwit some stingy townspeople who insist they have no food to share. This is one of those satisfying stories that lets readers feel in on the joke.

A Picture Book of Martin Luther King, Jr. by David A. Adler (Holiday House, 1989). This is one in a series of biographies for young readers. Some others are about Frederick Douglass, Sitting Bull, Sojourner Truth, Eleanor Roosevelt, George Washington, Helen Keller, Thomas Jefferson, and Abraham Lincoln.

CHAPTER 5: SEE THROUGH SOMEONE ELSE'S EYES

There's no reason to stick to a diet of royal personages, cuddly animals, or elves. Seek out books with unusual characters and viewpoints, whether made-up creatures or people from different cultures.

For Beginners

Harriet's Recital by Nancy Carlson (Carolrhoda, 1982). Harriet loves to dance, but has terrible stage fright. How does it feel to be Harriet on the eve of her big recital?

I Am an Artist by Pat Lowery Collins (Millbrook Press, 1992). This charming book shows young readers how an artist looks at the world.

Just Me by Marie Hall Ets (Viking, 1965). A little girl imitates the animals she meets as she strolls around the family farm. This book practically begs the reader to do as the little girl does.

For Intermediate Readers

Bedtime for Frances by Russell Hoban (Harper Trophy, 1960). Frances, who also has adventures in five subsequent books, is an engaging young badger whose thoughts and actions may remind young readers of their own. In this book, to her parents' dismay, she really doesn't want to go to bed.

Crictor by Tomi Ungerer (Harper Collins, 1958). Crictor is a boa constrictor who happens to grow up in a French village in the home of Madame Bodot. What would it be like to be Crictor? How would you see the world?

I Am the Dog, I Am the Cat by Donald Hall (Dial, 1994). Two familiar

household pets have a conversation about their differences. Like a play, this is written in dialogue. (See Chapter 3, Tell the Difference)

For Advanced Readers

The 500 Hats of Bartholomew Cubbins by Dr. Seuss (Vanguard Press, 1965). A high and mighty king sees the world one way; lowly Bartholomew has another point of view. It's fun to look through both pairs of eyes.

Poetry for Young People by Carl Sandburg (Sterling, 1995). Among these striking poems for children are several that reflect unique points of view. See "Under a Telephone Pole," a poem told by a copper wire, "A Sphinx," told by you-know-who, and "Rat Riddles," in which the poet converses with a rat.

Two Bad Ants by Chris Van Allsburg (Houghton Mifflin, 1988). This wild adventure is told and illustrated entirely through the eyes of two fearless ants who are hunting for "white crystals" in a human's kitchen.

Charlotte's Web by E. B. White (Harper, 1952). You cannot have a bookshelf without a copy. Although you may think the book is too advanced for your child, in fact it has something to say to children of all ages, and grown-ups, too. A cast of well-defined human and animal characters provides many opportunities to see through others' eyes.

CHAPTER 6: READ BETWEEN THE LINES

Be on the lookout for opportunities to draw inferences from what you are reading. Go easy on the beginners; this is a skill that takes time to develop.

For Beginners

An Extraordinary Egg by Leon Lionni (Knopf, 1994). A frog discovers an egg and thinks that what pops out is a chicken. Read between the lines and use the pictures to discover what kind of animal it really is.

Peter's Chair by Ezra Jack Keats (HarperCollins, 1967). Peter has a brand new baby sister, and life at home just isn't the same. Infer how Peter feels about this turn of events and how his feelings come to change.

For Intermediate Readers

Alexander and the Dragon by Katharine Holabird (Clarkson N. Potter, 1988). A child who's afraid of the dark sees a dragon under the bed. Do his parents believe him? Do you?

The Great Pig Escape by Eileen Christelow (Clarion, 1994). Five pigs run away from Bert and Ethel's farm. That same day, some clothes mysteriously disappear. Is there a connection? There is if you read between the lines.

My Dad, The Magnificent by Kristy Parker (Puffin, 1987). One little boy boasts about his fireman father's heroism. The other fibs to make his businessman father sound just as brave. If you read carefully, you will discover why the second father is outstanding in his own quiet way.

For Advanced Readers

My Wicked Stepmother by Norman Leach (MacMillan, 1993). Tom hates his dad's new wife. He thinks she's literally a witch. Is she as horrible as Tom tells us she is? Use your powers of deduction to decide if Tom is right or wrong.

Katie's Trunk by Ann Turner (MacMillan, 1992). This is set during the American Revolution and based on a true story from the writer's family. When American rebels break into young Katie's home, she hides in her mother's wedding trunk. There's lots hidden between the lines as Katie hears the rebels coming closer and closer.

Sarah, Plain and Tall by Patricia MacLachlan (Harper Trophy, 1985). A new classic, this is one of those books that appeals to children in different ways at different ages. A widower with two young children woos a new wife by mail. What can we infer about Sarah, the children's mother-to-be, from her letters?

CHAPTER 7: GET THE POINT

This skill applies to practically everything you read.

For Beginners

Frederick by Leo Lionni (Pantheon, 1967). All summer long, a family of mice gathers food for the winter—all except Frederick, who gathers ideas, colors, and feelings. Come winter, when days are long and bleak, Frederick, a poet, shows the fruits of his labor. The idea here is that there are many ways of doing your share.

Think of a Beaver by Karen Wallace (Candlewick Press, 1993). Learn all about beavers and pick out the most important facts about them.

Watch Where You Go by Sally Noll (Greenwillow, 1990). A tiny mouse's trip through the jungle is full of hidden dangers. What looks like wavy grass is really a lion's mane; what appears to be a vine is really a snake. The main idea is in the title!

For Intermediate Readers

Brothers and Sisters by Ellen B. Sinisi (Scholastic, 1993). Children will get the point right away. These captioned photographs celebrate having a brother or sister around the house.

Dandelion by Don Freeman (Viking, 1964). Dandelion, who happens to be a lion, decides to get all spruced up for Jennifer Giraffe's party. However, when he gets to her house, she doesn't recognize him in his silly new hairdo and fussy clothes. The author concludes that it's always best to be yourself.

William's Doll by Charlotte Zolotow (HarperCrest, 1972). A little boy can't be talked out of wanting a doll. Fortunately, his grandmother understands why it's a fine idea: He can practice being a father.

For Advanced Readers

Feel the Wind by Arthur Doros (Crowell, 1989). Almost every page of this informative book about air has an idea worth remembering.

Hani and the Tree Huggers by Jeannine Atkins (Lee & Low Books, 1995). Based on a real event, this is the story of how a group of brave women in a village in India banded together to save a grove of trees. Their action expresses the idea that nature is more precious than gold.

The Three Wishes: An Old Story by Margot Zemach (Farrar, Straus & Giroux, 1986). A woodcutter and his wife are granted three wishes. While they do not get what they think they want, they learn two important lessons: be careful what you wish for, and be happy with what you have.

CHAPTER 8: SPARK THE IMAGINATION

Some books tell you everything you need to know. Others serve as perfect springboards for imagination, pointing young readers down the path to fantasy.

For Beginners

Corduroy by Don Freeman (Viking, 1968). A department store teddy bear who is missing a button on his jumper is rejected by a customer. That night, Corduroy wanders around the store searching for his lost button. Imagine what you'd do if you were all alone in a big department store all night.

Let's Pretend by Dessie and Chevelle Moore (HarperFestival, 1994). A beginner's make-believe book: Let's pretend to run a store, make a cake, drive a car . . .

Night Ride by Bernie and Mati Karlin (Simon & Schuster, 1988). Mother drives her car at night, talking with the boy beside her. Imagine who they are, where they are coming from, and how they happen to be on the road so late . . .

For Intermediate Readers

Goodnight Opus by Berkeley Breathed (Little, Brown, 1993). Little Opus loves to hear Grandma read his favorite book, "Goodnight, Room," over and over again. But after hearing it for the 210th time, Opus thinks up a different ending. See what Opus comes up with, and invent your own adventures. This is a great antidote for the parent who's been asked to read *Goodnight, Moon* too many times!

Isabella's Bed by Alison Lester (Houghton Mifflin, 1993). Two children are transported to far-away places when they sleep in Isabella's bed. Imagine where you would go.

Outside Over There by Maurice Sendak (Harper Trophy, 1981). Papa is at sea and Little Ida, who plays the French horn, is minding baby sister. When goblins steal the infant, leaving an ice-baby in her place, Little Ida plunges into a land of fantasy and adventure to find the kidnappers and rescue her sister. A great starting point for day-dreaming.

For Advanced Readers

The Care and Feeding of Fish by Sarjo Frieden (Houghton Mifflin, 1996). Loulou gets an unusual fish as a pre-sent. Together, they go out on the town. Think of all the things you could do with a magical pet.

Space Case by Edward Marshall (Puffin, 1980). An extraterrestrial lands on earth on Halloween night and falls in with a bunch of trick-or-treaters. Buddy invites the thing home and takes it to school and then waves it off to Jupiter. Talk about science fiction and ask your young reader to concoct her own adventure in outer space.

The Stranger by Chris Van Allsburg (Houghton Mifflin, 1986). Van Allsburg's haunting books always keep readers guessing. In this story, a mysterious stranger comes to live on the Bailey farm. Your child can imagine who the stranger is and why he seems to have an odd connection to the changing seasons.

CHAPTER 10: THINK IT OVER

Think in twos, or even threes. Look for books that go together.

Ali Baba and the Forty Thieves retold by Walter McVitty (Harry N. Abrams, 1988) can be compared with the story of Aladdin (Chapter 5) as they are both tales of poor young men who make their fortune in different ways. Next, compare the original Aladdin with the Walt Disney version. (Intermediate / Advanced)

Cowboy Dreams by Dayal Kaur Khalsa (Dragonfly, 1990) is the story of a little girl who wants to be a cowboy and creates a make-believe range in her city home by riding a banister instead of a horse. How does her vision of cowgirl life differ from Glen Round's story of home on the range (Chapter 7)? (Beginner/Intermediate)

The Egyptian Cinderella by Shirley Climo (HarperCollins, 1989) is one of the world's oldest Cinderella stories. It is based on the life of a real slave girl who became the wife of a Pharaoh about 2500 years ago. Think about Cinderella when you read this version, in which the falcon-god Horus drops the slave girl's slipper into the Pharaoh's lap. (Intermediate /Advanced)

In *The Monster Bed* by Jeanne Villis and Susan Varley (Lothrop, Lee & Shepard, 1986), a baby monster tells his mother (in rhyme) that he's afraid there's a human under his bed. Alexander of *Alexander and the Dragon* (see *Really Reading!* Bookshelf, Chapter 6) would surely understand. So would the little badger in *Bedtime for Frances* (see *Really Reading!* Bookshelf, Chapter 5). (Beginner/ Intermediate)

Julius, The Baby of the World by Kevin Henkers (Greenwillow, 1990) drives his big sister nuts. The little boy in Charlotte Zolotow's *If It Weren't for You* (Harper & Row, 1966) finds his brother just as much of a pain. Find the similarities and differences between these books. (Beginner /Intermediate)

Petunia by Roger Duvoisin (Knopf, 1958) is a foolish goose who thinks just carrying a book around the barnyard will make her wise. Remember Winnie, the silly hen in *Wings* (Chapter 6)? (Intermediate)

After reading the myth of Ta-aroa (Chapter 4), pick up *Raven: A Trickster Tale from the Pacific Northwest* by Gerald McDermott (Harcourt Brace, 1993), a Native American myth about how Raven stole the sun and gave it to human beings. (Advanced)

The Three Billy Goats Gruff (see *Really Reading!* Bookshelf, Chapter 4) had to outsmart the big ugly troll who guarded the bridge to green pastures. In the *Toll-Bridge Troll* by Patricia Rae Wolff (Harcourt Brace, 1995), a schoolboy is faced with a similar problem. (Beginner /Intermediate)

Wonderful Worms (Chapter 7) introduced beginners to the busy world beneath our feet. *Under the Ground* (Scholastic, 1990) digs deeper, going beyond worms to beetles, moles, badgers, ants and other animals who make their homes underground. (Beginner/Intermediate)

Books Discussed

CHAPTER 1: GUESS WHAT HAPPENS NEXT!

For Beginners

The Story of Ferdinand by Munro Leaf (Puffin, 1936)

The Tale of Peter Rabbit by Beatrix Potter (Frederick Warne, 1902)

The Three Little Pigs. Of the many versions in print, one of our favorites is by James Marshall (Dial, 1989).

The Very Lonely Firefly by Eric Carle (Philomel, 1995)

For Intermediate Readers

"The Elephant's Child" is just one of the *Just So Stories* by Rudyard Kipling (Doubleday, 1912). There is also a fine new edition illustrated by Michael Foreman (Viking, 1987).

The Paperbag Princess by Robert Munsch and illustrated by Michael Martchenko (Annick Press, 1980).

For Advanced Readers

Mrs. Piggle-Wiggle's Magic by Betty MacDonald (Harper Trophy, 1985)

Pinocchio: The Sstory of a Puppet. The original version, by Carlo Collodi, is widely available. There is also a beautifully illustrated adaptation for younger readers by Ed Young (Philomel, 1996).

CHAPTER 2: WHAT DOES THIS MEAN?

For Beginners

Goldilocks and the Three Bears is one story you won't have to look far to find. Try Tomie dePaola's *Favorite Nursery Tales* (Putnam's Sons, 1986).

For Intermediate Readers

Horton Hatches the Egg by Dr. Seuss (Random House, 1940, renewed 1968)

Sundiata: Lion King of Mali by David Wisniewski (Houghton Mifflin, 1992)

Sylvester and the Magic Pebble by Wiliam Steig (Simon & Schuster, 1969)

For Advanced Readers

"I Hear America Singing" by Walt Whitman in *The Golden Treasury of Poetry* (Golden Press, 1974)

James and the Giant Peach by Roald Dahl (Knopf, 1961, renewed 1989)

Mummies Made in Egypt by Aliki (Crowell, 1979)

CHAPTER 3: TELL THE DIFFERENCE

For Beginners

Before I Go to Sleep by Thomas Hood and illustrated by Maryjane Begin-Callanan (Putnam, 1990)

A single edition of "The Town Mouse and the Country Mouse" has been adapted by Janet Stevens (Holiday House, 1987). For this fable and more, see *The Aesop for Children* (Scholastic, 1994) or *Aesop's Fables: A Classic Illustrated Edition* (Chronicle, 1990).

For Intermediate Readers

The Legend of Sleepy Hollow by Washington Irving, retold and illustrated by Will Moses (Philomel Books, 1995)

For Advanced Readers

Teammates by Peter Golenbock (Harcourt Brace Jovanovich, 1990)

Wild and Woolly Mammoths by Aliki (Harper Trophy, 1983)

CHAPTER 4: SAY IT IN YOUR OWN WORDS

For Beginners

The Little Red Hen by Byron Barton (HarperCollins, 1993) is one stand-alone version. The tale is also found in Tomie de Paola's *Favorite Nursery Tales* (Putnam, 1996).

Make Way for Ducklings by Robert McClosky (Viking, 1941, renewed 1969)

For Intermediate Readers

In the Beginning: Creation Stories from Around the World by Virginia Hamilton (Harcourt Brace Jovanovich, 1988)

"The Shepherd Boy and Wolf," one of Aesop's *Fables*, is retold by Tony Ross, (Dial, 1985). There is also a paperback adaptation by Ann McGovern (Scholastic, 1963). This fable is also known as "The Boy Who Cried Wolf" and "The Wolf and the Shepherd."

For Advanced Readers

Rachel Carson by William Accorsi (Holiday House, 1993)

CHAPTER 5: SEE THROUGH SOMEONE ELSE'S EYES

For Beginners

"Cinderella" has been retold many times and is included in *The Rainbow Fairy Book*, a collection of classic fairy tales edited by Andrew Lang (William Morrow, 1993). If you prefer a single edition, see *Cinderella, or the Little Glass Slipper*, the Charles Perrault version translated by Marcia Brown (Scribner's, 1954).

"Jack and the Beanstalk" can be found in many collections of children's stories, such as *Favorite Nursery Tales* (Putnam, 1986).

The True Story of the 3 Little Pigs! By A. Wolf as told to Jon Scieszka and illustrated by Lane Smith (Viking Penguin, 1989) tells the wolf's side of the story. Compare it with the version told by James Marshall (Dial, 1989), who clearly believes that the pigs were telling the truth.

For Intermediate Readers

The Escape of Marvin the Ape by Caralyn and Mark Buehner (Dial, 1992)

"The Tale of Aladdin and the Wonderful Lamp" can be found in the classic *Aladdin and Other Tales from the Arabian Nights*, (Knopf, 1993). Carrol Carrick has adapted a fine version (Scholastic, 1989).

Thumbelina, by Hans Christian Andersen, has been retold by Amy Ehrlich and illustrated by Susan Jeffers (Puffin, 1979). This story and other tales by Andersen are in the beautifully illustrated *Fairy Tales of Hans Christian Andersen* (Viking, 1995).

For Advanced Readers

Alexander and the Terrible, Horrible, No Good, Very Bad Day by Judith Viorst (Atheneum, 1972)

Through Grandpa's Eyes by Patricia MacLachlan (Harper & Row, 1979)

CHAPTER 6: READ BETWEEN THE LINES

For Beginners

Hansel and Gretel is included in the *Rainbow Fairy Book*, edited by Andrew Lang (William Morrow, 1993) as well as in *A Treasury of Children's Literature* (Ariel, 1992).

"Humpty Dumpty" is included in almost every collection of *Mother Goose Rhymes*. Two of the best editions are *The Random House Book of Mother Goose Rhymes*, selected and illustrated by Arnold Lobel (Random House, 1986) and *A Treasury of Mother Goose*, illustrated by Hilda Offen (Simon & Schuster, 1984).

The Princess and the Pea, by Hans Christian Andersen, is available in a single edition with elegant illustrations by Dorothee Duntze (North-South Books, 1984).

The Runaway Bunny by Margaret Wise Brown (HarperCollins, 1972)

The Story of Ferdinand by Munro Leaf (Puffin, 1936)

For Intermediate Readers

The Little Engine that Could retold by Walty Piper (Platt & Munk, 1984)

The New King by Doreen Rappaport (Dial, 1995)

Wings: A Tale of Two Chickens by James Marshall (Puffin, 1986)

For Advanced Readers

"The Night Before Christmas" (also known as "A Visit of St. Nicholas"), by Clement C. Moore, can be found in *A Treasury of Children's Literature* (Ariel, 1992), in Diane Goode's *Christmas Magic: Poems and Carols* (Random House, 1992), and in single editions that come out every Christmas.

The Emperor's New Clothes, by Hans Christian Andersen, is retold by Freya Littledale (Four Winds, 1980). This story is also included in the award-winning *Hans Christian Andersen Fairy Tales*, translated by Anthea Bell (Picture Book Studio, 1991).

Snow White and the Seven Dwarfs, by the Brothers Grimm, was adapted for the Walt Disney Company by Lisa Ann Marsoli. A new edition of the original tale has been brilliantly illustrated by Chalres Santore (Park Lane Press, 1996).

CHAPTER 7: GET THE POINT

For Beginners

Caps for Sale: A Tale of a Peddler, Some Monkeys and Their Monkey Business, by Esphyr Slobodkina (Harper Trophy, 1987)

Cowboys by Glen Rounds (Holiday House, 1991)

Wonderful Worms by Linda Glaser (Millbrook Press, 1992)

For Intermediate Readers

"King Midas" can be found in *Realms of Gold: Myths and Legends from around the World*, written by Ann Pilling and Illustrated by Kady MacDonald Denton (Kingfisher Books, 1993) and in many other collections and stand-alone versions.

"The Owl" is taken from *A Child's Treasury of Poems* edited by Mark Daniel (Dial, 1986).

"The Swallow" by Christina Rossetti appears in *The Golden Treasury of Poetry*, selected by Louis Untermeyer (Golden Press, 1959).

For Advanced Readers

Mona Lisa: The Secret of the Smile by Letizia Galli (Doubleday, 1996)

CHAPTER 8: SPARK THE IMAGINATION

For Beginners

Goldilocks and the Three Bears retold by David McPhail (Scholastic, 1995)

Sleeping Beauty retold by Trina Schart Hyman (Little, Brown, 1977)

The Tale of Peter Rabbit by Beatrix Potter (Frederick Warne, 1902)

For Intermediate Readers

Hansel and Gretel as told by Sheila Black (Citadel Press, 1994) comes with a bonus: Flip the book over and find the witch's side of the story.

Horton Hatches the Egg by Dr. Seuss (Random House, 1940, renewed 1968)

Peacock Pie by Thomas Hood (USA: Holt, 1969; Canada: Faber and Faber, 1970)

The Secret in the Matchbox by Val Willis (Farrar, Straus & Giroux, 1988)

The Stupids Step Out written by Harry Allard and illustrated by James Marshall (Houghton Mifflin, 1974)

For Advanced Readers

"Jabberwocky" may be found in *Through the Looking Glass*, by Lewis Carroll.

The Little Match Girl by Hans Christian Andersen (Putnam, 1990) is in many collections of Andersen fairy tales. There is also a version for younger readers retold by Erin Augenstine (Ariel, 1992).

The Wreck of the Zephyr by Chris Van Allsburg (Houghton Mifflin, 1983)

CHAPTER 9: BE A WRITER

For Beginners

"A List" is one of four stories in *Frog and Toad Together* by Arnold Lobel (Harper & Row, 1971)

A Snowy Day by Ezra Jack Keats (Viking Penguin, 1962, 1990)

For Intermediate Readers

Father Fox's Pennyrhymes by Clyde Watson (Harper Collins, 1971)

For Advanced Readers

The Jolly Postman by Janet Allan Ahlberg (Little, Brown, 1986)

CHAPTER 10: THINK IT OVER

For Beginners

I Wish I Were a Lion, by Eve Tharlet (North-South Books, 1993)

I Wish I Were a Mouse by Eve Tharlet (North-South Books, 1993)

I Wish I Were a Baby by Eve Tharlet (North-South Books, 1994)

I Wish I Were a Bird by Eve Tharlet (North-South Books, 1994)

For Intermediate Readers

The Escape of Marvin the Ape by Caralyn and Mark Buehner (Dial, 1992)

"How the Ostrich Got Its Long Neck: A Tale from the Akamba of Kenya," retold by Verna Aardema (Scholastic, 1995)

Paco and the Witch: A Puerto Rican Folktale retold by Felix Pitre (Dutton, 1995)

Rumplestiltskin by the Brothers Grimm, retold by Paul O. Zelinsky (Dutton, 1986)

For Advanced Readers

"Paul Revere's Ride," by Henry Wadsworth Longfellow, is included in *A Child's Anthology of Poetry* (Ecco Press, 1995)

A Picture Book of Paul Revere by David Adler (Holiday House, 1989)

The Pied Piper of Hamelin (poem) by Robert Browning (Knopf, 1993)

The Pied Piper of Hamelin is retold by Deborah Hautzig (Random House, 1989). See also Sara and Stephen Corrin's prose version (Harcourt Brace Jovanovich, 1989)

Spell board —

Ruth Brown
Carle